NEVER FAR
FROM HOME

NEVER FAR FROM HOME

My Journey from Brooklyn
to Hip Hop, Microsoft,
and the Law

BRUCE JACKSON

ATRIA BOOKS

NEW YORK LONDON TORONTO SYDNEY NEW DELHI

ATRIA
BOOKS

An Imprint of Simon & Schuster, Inc.
1230 Avenue of the Americas
New York, NY 10020

The names and identifying characteristics of some individuals have been changed. Some dialogue has been re-created.

"One Thousand Nine Hundred and Sixty-Eight Winters" by Jackie Earley reprinted by permission of the author.

First Atria Books hardcover edition February 2023

ATRIA BOOKS and colophon are trademarks of Simon & Schuster, Inc.

For information about special discounts for bulk purchases, please contact Simon & Schuster Special Sales at 1-866-506-1949 or business@simonandschuster.com.

The Simon & Schuster Speakers Bureau can bring authors to your live event. For more information or to book an event, contact the Simon & Schuster Speakers Bureau at 1-866-248-3049 or visit our website at www.simonspeakers.com.

Interior design by Timothy Shaner, NightandDayDesign.biz

Manufactured in the United States of America

1 3 5 7 9 10 8 6 4 2

Library of Congress Cataloging-in-Publication Data
Names: Jackson, Bruce (Lawyer), author.
Title: Never far from home : my journey from Brooklyn to Hip Hop, Microsoft, and the law / Bruce Jackson.
Description: First Atria Books hardcover edition. |
New York, NY : Atria Books, 2023.
Identifiers: LCCN 2022037019 (print) | LCCN 2022037020 (ebook) |
ISBN 9781982191153 (hardcover) | ISBN 9781982191160 (paperback) |
ISBN 9781982191177 (ebook)
Subjects: LCSH: Jackson, Bruce (Lawyer) | Corporate lawyers—United States—Biography. | African American lawyers—Biography. | Microsoft Corporation—Biography.
Classification: LCC KF373.J327 A3 2023 (print) | LCC KF373.J327 (ebook) | DDC 340.092 [B]—dc23/eng/20220924
LC record available at https://lccn.loc.gov/2022037019
LC ebook record available at https://lccn.loc.gov/2022037020

ISBN 978-1-9821-9115-3
ISBN 978-1-9821-9117-7 (ebook)

To my mother, Flora Mae Miller, my grandmother Mamie Jackson, and my aunt Viola Jackson, for being my inspiration and pushing me harder when I doubted myself.

To my children, Sabree, Maya, Kayla, and Corey, for being my continuous motivation.

To my late aunt Ceola Harvell and the late Ray "Spanky" Middleton, for their support.

CONTENTS

FOREWORD

Each of us lives a life that presents multiple paths. There are paths we choose to take. There are paths we reject in favor of others. There are paths we dream about that are open to others but not ourselves. And there are paths that we didn't dream possible, but, sometimes and somehow, they become true.

Bruce Jackson's life is a captivating journey that takes all these paths.

It's a life that sheds light on what it was like to grow up poor and Black in New York City. He confronted everyday hardships, including crime on the streets. And one day, at the age of ten, he found himself running from police through a Brooklyn subway station.

Bruce ran not from a crime he had committed, but out of fear after being mistaken in a crowd for someone else. Driven more by terror than thought, his path led him to jump onto the track in front of a subway train, where he managed to hop over the electrified third rail.

The path that is his life story could have ended then and there. But having met Bruce later in his life, I'll always be thankful it did not.

The journey from that subway station to Microsoft, where I first met Bruce, was far from a straight line. In many ways, his journey was different from my own path as I grew up in northeastern Wisconsin. But Bruce's life offers many lessons for all of us, regardless of our personal circumstances.

For a time, Bruce followed a path that took him to a part-time clerical job in the basement of the Chase Manhattan Bank in lower Manhattan when he was a high school student. Anyone playing the odds might have bet that Bruce would join the ranks of the other clerical workers who started then and who are still working there decades later. But, as Bruce writes, sometimes it's critical to "realize what you don't want out of life, which can be almost as important as figuring out what you do want."

Bruce's journey involved not just broader ambitions but also a lot of help from others. Never far from home, the intervening wisdom and constant support of his mother, grandmother, and aunt played critical roles in helping him become the first in his family to attend college. But his arrival as a freshman at Hofstra University's lush campus was far from a walk in the park. The academics were difficult and the culture daunting. Bruce's path almost took a U-turn back to a clerical job in Manhattan.

Bruce's journey has involved not just twists and turns, but also ups and downs. His first years at Microsoft speak poignantly to the loneliness of working in Seattle two decades ago at a company that was only beginning to diversify its workforce. He provides powerful insights into what it's like to work as a Black professional when almost everyone around you is white.

Our two paths started to connect more closely in 2002, when Bruce decided he wanted to move from Seattle back to the East Coast. I helped him identify a path within Microsoft's legal department that would bring him home to New York and into growing success in hammering out complex contracts with the company's largest customers. As he rose to more senior positions, I frequently benefitted from his advice, not only on legal and business issues, but also on what we needed to do to build a more supportive environment for a more diverse workforce.

Despite Bruce's success, in multiple ways he has continued to live a life that has lived up to this book's title, *Never Far from Home*. As I learned over the years, he lives this mantra, supporting family and friends, and by playing a growing role in community groups in New York and acting as a mentor for others.

At the same time, part of Bruce's journey has involved the continuing and painful prejudices directed at so many Black Americans. I vividly remember the story he recounts in the prologue, which he shared with me after it happened. Despite his years of success, failure to pay a simple parking ticket (incurred by someone else) led to Bruce's arrest, when he was put into handcuffs and leg irons and spent a night in jail. I have learned enough to appreciate that Bruce's experience that day was far from unique. In that sense, perhaps it wasn't even surprising. But it still felt shocking—and it should be for all of us.

Ultimately, Bruce's journey is a story of hope born from personal determination. One thing I have appreciated and even loved about Bruce is his constant willingness to be honest and direct. He shares advice even when it is difficult to hear, and always with an eye toward discovering a better solution. He seeks out and spends time sharing the personal details about other people that make it possible to understand more clearly how we can help them succeed.

All of this comes through in the book. The pages turn quickly. Bruce's life and story are a source of inspiration. Certainly for me. And I believe they will be for everyone.

Brad Smith
Vice Chair and President
Microsoft Corporation

NEW YORK, 2010

The Amsterdam Houses never change. The sprawling housing project comes into view as I make the familiar left turn from Eleventh Avenue onto Sixty-First Street and climb uphill from Manhattan's west side. The Houses are a city within a city: nine acres, more than a thousand residents, and countless stories that never see the light of day. The mass of brick towers feels as foreboding as ever—bad enough for me when I get pulled back for an extended residency every few years, but worse still for my mother, who remains as stuck to this place as the memories of my youth on the edge. This time, I've been brought back by the twin traumas of an imploding marriage and a house fire that has rendered uninhabitable my home in Mount Vernon, New York.

But this place is home, always will be. To me and countless friends and relatives here and gone, too many now lost to drugs and violence and crime. Yesterday, a Sunday, I broke bread with some of the folks in this neighborhood and joined with them in prayer at Sunday service. Today, my team closed a hundred-million-dollar deal for Microsoft, where I've

1

worked for more than a decade. We held a party in the office to mark the win. Then I met a friend and drove to the grocery store to pick up a batch of crab legs and some beers—for a celebration party with family and friends.

Some people—and this is especially true of those who grew up poor—like to dig at their roots until they give way completely, and there is nothing to draw them back. Makes it easier to shape-shift into something else; to blend in at corporate functions or black-tie charity events.

I want to help these people. But don't get the wrong idea. I was never one of them.

Not me, but I get it. If you're uncomfortable with who and what you were, you want to pretend it never happened. But as far as I'm concerned, everything I've accomplished grew from the roots of the city and projects and distressed neighborhoods that raised me. The Houses are no less a part of me than the blood that flows through my veins. Hell, I'm proud of it. But I also know it could have turned out like it did for many of my friends: dead or incarcerated. Reality has a way of shaking me awake whenever I'm tempted to forget about that fact.

Right on cue: Blue and red lights dance kaleidoscopically in the rearview mirror, revealing the unmistakable outline of an NYPD cruiser. Then two quick burps of a siren, as if I hadn't already gotten the message. I pull my gray BMW X5 to the curb, cut the engine, and wait. Hands on the wheel. Ten and two. Eyes ahead. I am an attorney, so I know my rights. I am also a Black man in America, so I know the drill.

"Relax," I say to my passenger, an old friend, to my right. "It'll be okay."

Two officers, both fair-skinned, approach the vehicle. I roll down the window, try to remain calm. The officers are cordial but firm.

"Been following you since the bottom of the hill," one of them explains.

They say something is wrong with the taillight.

This is not true, but it falls under the vast umbrella of "probable cause." A taillight that *appears* to be flickering is as useful a tool to law enforcement, when so inclined, as blacked-out windows or a rumbling muffler. It is an excuse to detain, to intrude and violate. And so the dance begins. I turn over my license and registration. The officers retreat to their cruiser. Five minutes pass . . . ten . . . fifteen. By the time they return and declare flatly that "something" showed up on my license, and that they need to wait for their sergeant to report back, my friend skips from agitation straight to anger.

"This is bullshit!"

She may be right, but the outburst—continuous, peppered with expletives and accusations of racism—is not helping matters.

"You're just stopping him because he's a Black man."

"Ma'am, you keep running your mouth," one of the cops says, "I'm going to arrest you."

There is a standoff—the cop looks at me, with an unspoken *Get your friend under control*—before he walks away again. A crowd begins to gather on this pleasant spring night, ready for an unexpected show after dinner. Suddenly a backup patrol car hits the scene, and there are now four cops investigating an allegedly busted taillight. My hopes of a simple ticket and a talking-to are fading fast.

"Look," I say to my friend, "I think they're going to take me downtown. Maybe it's best if you leave."

"Leave?"

"Yeah. Take my keys and my car. Go home. I'll stay with the cops. Let's not make this any worse than it is. I'll be okay."

The officer strolls back over to the driver's side window. After a brief discussion, my friend is allowed to leave, right before I am handcuffed and placed in the back seat of a cruiser. More will be revealed in due time, they promise, but for now, *There is a problem with your license* is all I'll get.

First stop: Twentieth Precinct, West Eighty-Second Street. I am placed in a holding area with four other men and then moved to a cell all my own.

"Want a newspaper?" one officer asks.

"Sure. Thanks."

Time passes. Time to think about the fact that it's been nearly forty years since the last time I found myself in this situation, detained by law enforcement. So much has changed in my life, and apparently, so little. The officer returns. There are two women outside, he explains, and they aren't happy. He tells me their names—Adrienne and Diane. One, my friend and passenger from earlier, the other, my sister. They arrived together at the Twentieth Precinct to raise hell.

"Do me a favor," I say. "Tell them I'm sleeping."

He laughs. "Sleeping?"

"Yeah, if they think I'm comfortable and not bothered by this, that will put them at ease."

He shrugs, leaves, returns a while later. "They're gone. Guess you were right."

It is close to midnight when my attorney, Paul Martin, shows up. By this time, I have been informed of the charges—driving with a suspended license. Apparently my brother had picked up a parking ticket while driving my car and had failed to pay the fine. This transgression was news to me, but it was my responsibility, since the ticket was attached to a vehicle registered in my name.

Fair enough, but the truth is that no one—or almost no one—spends any time at all behind bars for nonpayment of a parking ticket or even a suspended license. The US judicial system is already choked to the point of immobility without tossing parking tickets into the blender. Typically, this kind of infraction merits a desk ticket and a future date with the state on the court docket. But, of course, justice is not blind, and here I am, a middle-aged man with a career on the rise and no criminal record, suddenly thrown into the system.

"Prints didn't come back yet," Paul says glumly.

I nod, knowing exactly what this means. If fingerprints don't clear the system by midnight, you're spending the night in jail.

"Hang in there," he says. "I'll see you tomorrow."

Moments later I am in handcuffs again, and leg irons, one of four men chained together, shuffling out a back door. They load us into a van and drive us uptown, to 126th Street, home of the Twenty-Sixth, a larger and more heavily staffed precinct. More cops. More cells. More criminals. We pass through metal door after metal door, the deafening CLANG of each a reminder of the fading light and intensifying odor as we fall deeper into the system.

I can feel my heart race. This is not exactly Rikers Island, but make no mistake—the tone and tenor of this facility shares little with my time reading a newspaper at the comparatively genteel Twentieth Precinct. The sense of dread is palpable. The four of us are divided and placed in different cells, all within view of one another. There is one other occupant in mine, a man who appears to be in his early thirties, wearing a ragged T-shirt and jeans. He is sprawled out on the cell's only bench, snoring away. I stand at the door, leaning against the bars, wondering how long I'll be here, how I got here. Until this night, I've never spent a minute behind bars, but I know enough about the streets and jailhouse protocol to know that if I stand here all night, peering out of the cell like a puppy in a kennel, a couple bad things will happen. One, I'll be exhausted. Two, I'll become a target in the eyes of my cellmate and anyone else who might join us later.

"Yo, man," I say as I walk to the bench. "Wake up."

The guy moans, rolls over, looks at me through dead eyes. He says nothing.

"I'm tired, too," I say. "I can't stand here all night. You gotta move over and give me some room."

He nods, sits up, and slides to the end of the bench. Then curls into himself again. I take a seat at the other end and begin my fight with the anxiety of incarceration. My chest is tight, my throat dry. Suddenly I am nearly overcome with the urge to scream, to let everyone within earshot know that *I DON'T BELONG HERE!* My hands are clammy. The room is spinning.

Get a grip, I tell myself. *It isn't that bad, you'll be out in the morning.* But the lack of control is terrifying: the sense that I am buried deep within this maze of broken dreams and violence and no one gives a shit.

"Sandwich?"

There is an officer at the gate, passing out food, or something like it, anyway. Flattened slices of white bread wrapped in cellophane.

"No, thanks."

He holds out a bottled water. I consider it briefly. I'm thirsty, scared. But there is a single, open toilet in a corner of the cell, and anything that needs to leave my body will be doing so for an audience.

"Nah."

He shrugs, walks away.

I close my eyes and withdraw into a fantasy world: a meditative trance, of sorts. Summoning up a long-lost part of my past, from adolescent flirtations with the theater, I slip into character. In this scenario, I am not a criminal. I am a correspondent, working undercover; an intrepid investigative journalist rooting out inequities and racial injustice by placing himself on the front lines of the war. I tell myself that I am merely a visitor to this universe, not a resident. I am here to observe and report. I am here to learn.

And then go home.

It's all nonsense, but in a weird way it helps. After a while, my pulse slackens. My skin dries. I can breathe again. An hour passes, maybe two.

We are cuffed and chained together again, only this time there are eight of us, led out of the basement jail and into a waiting van. Accompanied fore and aft by NYPD patrol cars, we rumble down the West Side Highway beneath the cover of night, the city eerily still and quiet. There is a small window in the back of the vehicle, and through it I see the city lights flickering off the Hudson, splashing fingers of yellow and orange across the black water. A few of the guys around me manage to fall asleep, even as the van bobs and weaves along the rutted highway. We are on our way to Central Booking, stop number three on the night, and I can't help but think about the fact that absolutely no one who cares about me has any idea where I am at this moment. But I'm lucky: at least I know they're out there somewhere, friends and family who love me and who would be horrified to see me like this. I wonder if the same can be said of my fellow travelers.

Central Booking, 100 Centre Street, is a sprawling short-term lockup and courthouse in Lower Manhattan that serves as a way station for hundreds of inmates as they are fed into one of the penal system's many tributaries. If you get to Central Booking, the thinking goes, you probably did . . . *something*. The holding cells are bigger, nastier, louder. The guards and officers are tougher, more cynical.

I am tossed into a cage with roughly a dozen other men, most of whom appear to be half my years (forty-eight). But it's easier this time, even with a crowd. It's the middle of the night, but I walk over, tap one of the kids on the back, and tell him to make room. He grunts, moves down. I take a seat.

"The fuck you doin' here, old man?" one of them says to me.

"I ain't that old."

He laughs. The conversation ends. Everyone in jail is innocent, but I see no reason to explain myself. It's not going to help my credibility, or enhance my safety, to tell anyone that I've been arrested for failing to pay a traffic ticket. Better to let them assume the worst.

Time passes. More food and water are offered and rejected. The sun rises, although I can't see it. Attorneys begin showing up, court-appointed mostly. They speak to clients, accompany them into the courtroom. It goes on like this for hours, a steady march of the accused and the arraigned. Some post bail and leave. Some see their cases dismissed. Quite a few remain on site or are shipped out to serve bids elsewhere or to wait for resolution of more complicated matters. My attorney, Paul, arrives midmorning. He's calm, reassuring.

"I've already spoken to the DA," he says. "They're going to dismiss the charges. You just have to pay the ticket, and a fine, and it all gets wiped away."

"That's it?"

"Well, you still have to go in front of the judge, acknowledge culpability—"

"It wasn't my ticket. I didn't even know about it."

He sighs. "Come on, Bruce. Doesn't matter."

"Uh-huh."

Soon, it's all over. I am one of a hundred or more people who will stand in front of the judge, a fleeting and forgotten face. A name on an impossibly long ledger. Outside, Paul and I shake hands and go our separate ways. He offers me a ride uptown, but I decline. I need some time alone to clear my head.

I walk across the street and grab a Big Mac at a McDonald's on Broadway, polish it off while walking through SoHo. Eventually, I hop on the subway heading north. It has never felt better, the rocking of the car, the clacking of the wheels against the rails. With the exception of college, law school, and a brief, uncomfortable stint in the Pacific Northwest, I've lived in and around New York City my entire life. Even on the bad days, it's home.

I exit at Lincoln Center, the stop nearest the Amsterdam Houses. By now it's almost noon. Still time to get into work and make something of the day. It's not until I'm standing in the shower, trying to wash away the stench of eighteen hours in limbo, that the anger and anxiety rise up within me. I feel it all again—the hopelessness. The vile conditions. The stench of urine, of vomit, of nicotine, of sweat. I gag, choke it back.

A few minutes later I am neatly dressed and walking out the front door of one of Manhattan's largest housing projects, briefcase in hand, on my way to Microsoft Corporation's New York headquarters on Sixth Avenue. I've thought about this juxtaposition more than a few times since moving back home—the distance from here to there, physically and metaphorically—but there is a new poignancy to it today. As I rise through the glistening complex on an elevator to my sixth-floor office, I am nearly broken by the weight of a secret life, of the burden that most of my colleagues cannot possibly understand. Politeness rules. Pleasantries are exchanged, small talk is made. I am overwhelmed by the urge to tell everyone what happened, to share the gory details of a life they can't imagine.

"This is what can happen," I want to say, "if you are a person of color." This is what *will* happen if we aren't all vigilant, aware, persistent. Things have changed, mostly for the better. I know that. When I started at Microsoft a decade earlier, I was the third Black person ever hired in the company's legal department. With diversity and inclusion high on the company agenda, those numbers have improved, and I've done my best to help the cause. But up here, in the ivory tower, it's easy to forget the truth: that when I leave this office, I am not a Microsoft executive.

I want to tell them where I spent the night. I want to explain exactly how my reality differs from theirs when I leave this office. But I don't. I put my head down and go to work, crunching numbers, reviewing contracts, vetting deals. Someday, maybe I'll tell them what happened.

Someday.

Chapter 1

FLORA MAE

Flora Mae Jackson grew up in prewar South Carolina, one of five children who all started working in the cotton fields before the age of ten, and for whom poverty and racism were facts of life. She used to tell us stories about the raids—gangs of marauding Klansmen ripping through neighborhoods, and how she and her friends learned to hide in the crawl spaces beneath their houses until the terrors went away.

"How often did this happen?" I once asked.

Often enough, she said, that it wasn't even a shock.

My mother's family concerned itself with survival over everything. Education is great, but such things take a back seat when simply breathing another day feels barely within reach. And survival meant work. Flora Mae dropped out before she got to middle school, as did most of her siblings, so she could put in even more hours in the fields. One of my aunts was married by the age of fourteen. My grandmother Mamie Jackson moved to Brooklyn around that same time, found work, and shortly thereafter my mother followed suit. But since my grandmother worked as a live-in housekeeper and did not have her own apartment, Flora Mae moved in with a cousin in Bedford-Stuyvesant.

Not long after, my mother began dating the man who would father my older brother, Robert, but she and he did not marry. She met and moved in with John Wesley Miller, father to me and three of my sisters. Another sibling followed, they eventually married, and this is where we rooted ourselves in an apartment in a Crown Heights brownstone. My father does not cut a strong figure in my memories of this time. He was something of a spectral presence, popping in on occasion but never staying for long. He had grown up in North Carolina, in a family of educators, but had fled the South with his mother when she became enthralled with the teachings of a prominent and controversial reverend and followed him and his growing congregation to New York. The exact nature of their relationship, like so many things about my father's history, was shrouded in mystery.

My mother ran our home, working tirelessly to take care of six kids between shifts at a peanut-packaging plant. She did her best to keep us all in line, but the truth is, she was badly outnumbered.

Into the void of a fatherless household stepped a man named Robert Richardson, who was the superintendent of another building in the neighborhood. This was the sort of thing that happened in a lot of African American families in that era (and still happens today). The father disappears, and someone else moves in to fill the space. Not always literally, but emotionally. That was Robert. He was the guy who seemed to be around a lot of the time, hanging out with us, fixing things around the apartment, taking us to Coney

Island on the weekend. He was not my father, and I knew it, and for a while I sort of resented him for thinking he might fill that role. But that was just sort of a preteen phase, and later in life Robert and I became much closer—he is, in fact, the man you'll see in most of my graduation photos over the years—from high school, college, and law school. And if you were to ask most of my siblings, they'd probably refer to him as their father—certainly he was more of a father to all of us than John Wesley Miller.

But around that time, to me, Robert was mainly just a guy who hung out at our house, part-time, trying to be more of a friend than a father, and easing some of my mother's burden. That was the deal with Robert. He was married to someone else and had five kids of his own—an entirely separate family and life in East Flatbush, twenty minutes away from Crown Heights. A guy can only handle so much. We knew he had another family, and his family, I suspect, knew about us.

Robert and my mother had met through Robert's brother, a suitor of a family friend. The exact parameters of Robert and Mom's relationship were never clear, nor what my mother expected out of it aside from companionship and financial help. I certainly don't think she expected that Robert would ever trade one family for another. But life is complicated. People form bonds for different reasons. They learn to cope and survive. It isn't always a fairy tale. He cared for my mother, and we all appreciated that, but we also knew it wasn't his place to be the disciplinarian in our home. That last point led to a few confrontations through the years, some worse than others, but fewer and fewer over time. As often as not, Robert would shrug and give up the fight quickly.

It all sounds a bit crazy now, but it seemed pretty normal to me at the time. There were seven of us crammed into a small apartment, and we depended on public assistance to make ends meet (my mother's job was far from sufficient), but you couldn't have told me I was poor. Not at that age. Our neighbors lived the same way, and for the most part it was not an unpleasant existence. I had plenty of friends, a place to sleep, food, and relatives who lived nearby. When you're seven or eight years old, that feels like enough.

While Crown Heights in the late '60s was hardly the gentrified stretch of cafés, condos, and Michelin-star-worthy restaurants it is today, neither was it a terrible place to live. If you had friends and family around, which I did in abundance, it kind of felt like any modest upbringing anywhere else. A neighborhood of brownstones, some clean and sturdy, some in disrepair. There were pockets of dirt and filth, to be sure, but there were trees as well. There were patches of green. There were sidewalks teeming with familiar faces, entire families hanging out on stoops, passing the time with conversation and human connection. There were barbecues and block parties, and there were "rent parties"—gatherings of the neighborhood in support of a family or families who for one reason or another couldn't meet that month's payment on their home. Five dollars here, ten there, twenty on occasion. We had each other's backs. At the end of the party, the problem would go away, at least for a little while. It was a judgment-free zone, built on a foundation of love and shared hardship. Most families knew what it was like to struggle to make ends meet, and there was comfort in knowing that you wouldn't be alone the next time.

In the sweltering summer months, you'd throw open all the windows and hope for a breeze or a thunderstorm. Failing that, a popped fire hydrant worked wonders. The barrier between indoors and outdoors melted somewhere around July, with people coming and going, conversations filtering through screens and out into the street.

We had one nineteen-inch black-and-white television for the entire apartment to share, but there was always more entertainment to be found right outside the door, on my own block. What danger there was outside (violence, drugs, crime) felt distant, mostly unreal, something the adults would talk about but keep far enough away to stay out of mind. Family provided security and the illusion of safety. My grandmother lived in Crown Heights, as did my aunt Viola, and one of my uncles. Kin, all within walking distance, all ready to lend an ear or a hand.

My cousins, despite being kept on tighter leashes than the kids in our home, were the ones who got us in trouble. They introduced me to gambling during my visits to their places. They loved throwing dice outside the house, but they weren't very good at it, and usually I returned home with more money than I had when I left. Just nickels, dimes, and quarters, but it felt good to leave with a pocketful of change. Sometimes my uncle would catch us playing and immediately break up the game.

"What did I tell you kids about throwing dice?!" he'd scream, as we scattered through the neighborhood. Whether he was motivated by a goal to impart much-needed wisdom, an attempt at moral guidance, or merely raging at the prospect of his kids wasting money, I don't know. But at the time, I was pretty sure it was about the wasting more than the playing.

In my memory, I was an easygoing little kid, but Aunt Viola assures me that is a fault of temporal distance. "You were horrible as a kid—if your mother wouldn't buy you something when you went to the store together, you'd throw a tantrum right there in front of everyone. You'd knock stuff off the shelves and scream and cry, just to protest."

In my defense, Aunt Viola always took it upon herself to set a higher standard of behavior than the one I was accustomed to at home. She was the family's disciplinarian, the one who would not hesitate to dole out a beating if you talked back or acted out of turn. Aunt Viola had the switch and the belt, and she wasn't shy about using them, especially when it came to our too-frequent attempts to skip school. We were drunk on our own mischievous-little-kid cleverness. After a "school day" spent running around the neighborhood, we'd show up at Aunt Viola's house, right at 3:00 p.m., thinking no one would be the wiser, and she'd be there waiting for us with towering omniscience.

"How was school?" she'd say.

"Great!"

A moment of hope.

"Y'all ain't smart enough to miss school! Now get your ass over here."

She would become one of the most influential people in my life—the family member who would call me on my bullshit. Honest, real, direct. I liked visiting her home because my cousin Phillip, her son, was one of my closest friends, but also because I liked the structure she demanded. The comfort of knowing that she cared. Even if she could be tough or terrifying, I never doubted that it came from a place of love.

I attended elementary school at PS 289. I was smart enough to do okay in class without working too hard, but that's not to say I was particularly focused or driven. School was more of a way to pass the day than a critical function in my life at that time.

Some of my friends were bused to schools at least five miles away, measures intended to level the playing field and provide greater access to better teaching and facilities—pathways to life-changing opportunities. Their families tended to be grateful, but the kids I knew didn't like it. It pulled them out of their comfort zones and threw them into *someone else's* environment. A place where they'd go from understood to, in their own way, marginalized. Othered. Observed.

In law school, years later, I would cross paths with one of those kids, David Green, now my best friend, who took the chance to get out of his neighborhood. He grew up in the Bronx, experiencing a childhood shaped by poverty much like mine. But after middle school, he utilized A Better Chance (ABC), a scholarship program that allowed low-income families in academically challenged neighborhoods to send their kids to high-achieving boarding, day, or public schools far outside their districts. Instead of funneling into DeWitt Clinton High School alongside his friends and classmates, he left the Bronx for high school in a leafy Massachusetts suburb. At the time, he said, he resented the move. He'd had friends. He thought he'd figure things out and be okay. But his mother disagreed.

"It'll change your life," she said. "You're going."

The Georgetown Law diploma that hangs in his office today makes it hard to argue that point—but I have one of those, too. What I also have is a bond with my siblings and cousins and aunts and uncles that can only be developed through years of close proximity. There is a price to pay for uprooting yourself at that age. You set out at thirteen, never to return, and you lose something vital. There is regret, and there is anger. There is resentment toward a world that's telling you: *Your friends aren't good enough. Your teachers are inadequate. Your community—your people—are broken.*

We lived at 910 Prospect Place, a couple doors down from one of Crown Heights' hottest nightclubs, and on weekends I'd go outside with my friends and watch people coming and going, all dressed up. The club didn't look like much—just a single-story brownstone—but music from within would fill the street until late in the night. Other nights I'd lie in bed and listen, wondering what sort of magic happened inside that building. Imagination went a long way where I come from—after school we'd occupy ourselves with simple games played in the street. Ones that didn't require big, open fields or equipment we couldn't afford. Skelly, a kind of board game drawn in chalk on the pavement, where we'd advance by flipping bottle caps into designated squares. Or hot-peas-and-butter—a sadistic version of hide-and-seek you'd have to see to believe; the game would reach its frantic peak when someone got to chase everyone around, whipping them mercilessly with a leather belt until they'd found the sanctuary of home base.

Once a week or so, the Itchies, a street gang, would come by our neighborhood and shake down the younger kids for whatever meager cash or coins we might have.

We'd hear *"The Itchies are coming!"* and we'd all scatter. If you got caught and refused to give up your money, you'd get your ass kicked, or worse. I remember the school bully mistaking life on the street with his schoolyard domain and catching the point of an Itchy's blade one afternoon. Looking back, it feels almost quaint—street gangs running around and extorting money armed with nothing more formidable than a pocketknife. It didn't compare to the '80s and '90s, when guns became commonplace and you could be victimized by a drive-in just for being in the wrong place. To some degree, I was protected. If things ever got out of hand, I could go to my brother, who was seven years older and had some less-than-upstanding connections.

A certain moral code developed within me early, almost by osmosis. I learned to trust family and friends and to view warily anyone outside that circle. The white people I knew were considered interlopers, regardless of their intentions: teachers who commuted from Queens or Staten Island, nurses and doctors who lived in Manhattan or Brooklyn Heights.

Authority figures, law enforcement in particular, were deemed to be the enemy, an overwhelmingly white and aggressive occupying force in a neighborhood populated almost entirely by people of color.

At age six I barely noticed the tension; by ten I could feel it in my bones. I heard the rumble of dissent in conversations between adults. I saw it in the faces of older friends, who scattered when an NYPD patrol car turned a corner. Were they running because they had done something wrong . . . or because they were scared? I didn't know, and it didn't really matter. On our side, there was no expectation of fairness; on the other, no presumption of innocence. I knew this only in the abstract, but as I watched and listened and grew, it became more concrete. People were arrested. They went away. Sometimes they were beaten while being taken into custody.

Us versus them.

White versus Black.

Good guys and bad guys.

The confusion and dissonance could be overwhelming to a kid, and it even confuses adults now whenever I'm pressed on the matter. On one hand, you had friends and relatives who were, objectively speaking, on the wrong side of the law. But to us, the people who lived and played with them in the neighborhood, they were familiar. We watched them laugh, and boast, and mourn, and even cry. They treated us like equals. On the whole, they felt *less* threatening than the police officers whose jobs were ostensibly to protect us from those very same people. The cops were the ones who made you feel unwelcome on the sidewalk in front of your home, who put you on high alert at all times. Not the criminals who hung out in your midst. You ended up feeling more than a little conflicted. My friends did not want to become cops. I did not want to be a cop.

We all wanted to be like Black Sam.

With the benefit of experience and hindsight, I can now tell you that Sam was a pimp. A relative of ours (Sam's mother and my grandmother were sisters) who lived up in Boston but whose business interests periodically brought him back to New York. Every so often, he'd come to town with a couple of his girls; they'd do a hotel run, pile up customers, and crash for a few days before heading back home.

But as a kid, all of that wasn't so clear to me. What *did* I know about Sam? I knew that he dressed well, carried lots of money, always had a beautiful young woman by his side, and carried a gun. I met him for the first time at Aunt Viola's house. They were first cousins, and Sam was in town for one of his visits, mixing business and pleasure. I can still see him standing in the kitchen, lean and angular, smiling broadly as he extended a hand to say hello.

"Bruce, this is Sam," Aunt Viola said. "He's your cousin."

I didn't quite understand how someone nearly the same age as my mother could be a cousin, but familial terms like that were often tossed around loosely and without explanation. What mattered to me in that moment was the impact of Sam's presence. His appearance: the glistening, processed hair; the colorful one-piece jumpsuit opened to the sternum; the platform shoes! Sam looked like he could have stepped right off the set of *Soul Train*. He looked like a star. He looked . . . *important*.

"What's up, little man?" he said, extending a hand for me to shake. "I heard about you."

I stammered, smiled. Was this true? What had Aunt Viola told him? Was it good? Bad? Why did I care?

"Hello," I said. And nothing else. I was tongue-tied in his presence. With Sam that day was a woman named Lisa. She was younger than Sam and very pretty. He introduced her as "my girl." They were a couple, as surely and atypically as my mother and Robert were a couple. But they were also boss and employee, with Lisa turning tricks for Sam and Sam taking most of the money. As I got a little older, I began to see the reality of their alliance and to understand it, but I didn't dare pass judgment. No one did.

My interactions with Sam predate my teenage years, so they are colored by naivete. But I was old enough to get some sense of what he did for a living, and I knew that Sam was always the toast of the town when he came back. He'd throw parties, hand out money, sometimes have his girls perform favors on his friends (although not really "favors," as there were no freebies in Sam's business). I wasn't old enough for the parties or the girls, but I did think it was cool when Sam would greet me with a handful of cash. And I heard stories about Sam, about how he protected not just his girls but also his friends and family. If someone was short on the rent payment and Sam was in town, he'd make up the difference. You didn't mess with Sam, because if you did, he'd hurt you. He was a wiry little guy, but people both feared and admired him.

I do not mean to glorify the work of a pimp. I'm just being honest—to a bunch of poor city kids, Black Sam didn't feel like an outlaw. He was one of us—a kid from the projects (Roxbury, Massachusetts) who had figured things out and seemed to be doing well. Whatever moral or legal transgressions might have been involved, they were mostly irrelevant and mysterious. Did Sam exploit or abuse the girls in his employ? I didn't know any better. Did he ever kill anyone? A reasonable assumption, but I had no proof either way. Those things didn't concern us struggling to get by in Crown Heights. Here's what I do know: Sam went out like a gangster in every sense of the term, stabbed twenty-five times, bleeding out all over one of his fine, expensive suits in a New York hotel room.

He was barely thirty years old.

Chapter 2

"JUST TELL US YOU DID IT"

"This is the A train," my mother said as the subway screeched into view at the Fifty-Ninth Street station. "The express line to Brooklyn. Got it?"

"Uh-huh."

"When we get to Brooklyn, we'll switch to the C—that's the local. That's all you need to know—two trains, two stops."

I nodded. "Okay, Mommy."

"And don't talk to anyone," she added, her tone suddenly gentler, more concerned.

"Why not?"

"Because I said so. Just pay attention. Get to where you're going. You miss your stop, you'll end up in East New York."

"Where's that?"

"Never mind."

When we moved to the Amsterdam Houses in 1972, it felt like I'd just cashed in a winning lottery ticket. From the outside, it probably seems strange that moving from a Brooklyn brownstone to a housing project was a big step up, but it sure seemed that way. Suddenly we had more room and financial security—a three-bedroom apartment, utilities included, and . . . a working elevator!

I continued to spend a lot of time in Brooklyn, as my grandmother still lived there, and I had a bunch of friends and other relatives in the neighborhood. Sometimes my mother would go to my grandmother's house after work and stay the night. My grandmother was always willing to help, and even though we had moved to Manhattan, her apartment in Kingsborough Houses, a housing project in Crown Heights, remained something of a family nexus. So, at least once or twice a week, I'd meet my mother in Brooklyn after school.

Like most poor kids in New York, I learned to navigate the city on my own, memorizing the complex web of subway and bus routes. Even at ten years of age I thought nothing of venturing below the street alone and hopping on the subway, changing trains once or twice on the way to Crown Heights. It started out as an adventure. Then it became more utilitarian: simple transportation. I didn't even think about the risks. If I wanted to see Grandmama or my friends or cousins—if I wanted to go anywhere—I had to take public transportation. Simple as that. Like a goose imprinting the concept of migration on her chicks, my mother demonstrated the basics as soon as we moved to Manhattan, taking us into the labyrinthine subway system and making a forty-five-minute subterranean trip to Crown Heights seem as simple and unsophisticated as crossing the street.

Within a few weeks I had become an expert. It wasn't like I had a map of New York in my head—honestly, at that age I couldn't have told you whether I was heading north or south. I simply memorized the details of my trip and relied on the New York City Transit Authority to do the rest. To me, the subway was magical—you disappeared beneath the street and reappeared someplace else far away, as though teleported through time and space. It was glorious! But as my mother had tried to make clear, the subway was not without its dangers, and they could be found in unexpected places.

It was on one of these trips to my grandmother's house that I was arrested for the first time. I had come home from school at the customary time, hung out with some friends for a little while, and then walked to the Fifty-Ninth Street station around five o'clock, figuring I'd get to my grandmother's by six, just in time for dinner. The express train to Brooklyn was crowded, pretty typical for rush hour on a weekday. There weren't a lot of other kids on the train—mostly grown-ups on their way home from work—so I snaked my way through the human trees, working toward the front of the car, until I found an open seat. Today, of course, everyone retreats into their own little world when they utilize public transportation: eyes glued to the screens of their phones, earbuds pulsating with music. There is no human interaction, and any attempt at such is liable to be greeted with, at best, annoyance; at worst, hostility.

Leave me alone!

But in the 1970s, that miraculous bubble of isolation had yet to be invented. The subways were dirtier then, more dangerous, with graffiti-splashed trains whose lights flickered unreliably, sometimes casting nervous riders into darkness. A few people on the train—seasoned straphangers—read newspapers or paperbacks. Most just stared straight ahead, or out the window into the underground blackness. They scuffed their feet on the floor, perhaps kicking at imaginary interlopers. A few nodded off, their heads bobbing to the rhythm of the car. To me this was a show, almost as entertaining as the cartoons I watched on Saturday mornings. I glanced around the car, knowing instinctively that if someone returned my gaze, it was best to turn away.

Eventually the train pulled into the Utica Avenue station. I stood up and followed the flow of human traffic through the open doors and out onto the subway platform. The C train was maybe fifteen to twenty feet away, waiting on the other side of the platform. Both trains opened their doors to the middle; on the opposite side of each train, nearest the walls, the doors remained closed. By now we'd been living in Manhattan for at least six months. I'd made this trip, and this precise change of trains, at least twenty times. I could do it blindfolded. With my hands in my pockets, head down, I walked across the platform, daydreaming about dinner at Grandmama's house. Suddenly, I heard someone yell.

"There he is!"

You grow up fast in New York, especially in the parts of New York where I was raised, and you become immune to sights and sounds that might be alarming to those less seasoned in the ways of urban life. Yelling was not uncommon in New York, particularly in subway stations. They were crowded, cacophonous places, populated by a mix of the overburdened and the unwell. The sound of someone yelling might be nothing more than two people trying to connect; or it might be something more worrisome. I was cool enough to ignore it for the most part. But then, there it was again.

"Right over there. That one!"

I looked up and saw a police officer on the platform, talking to a man. I did not recognize the man, but he clearly was agitated. He waved his arms. Then he pointed in my direction.

"HIM!"

I looked at the man, red-faced, angry, and I felt fear rising in the back of my throat. I looked at the cop, a white man who was probably in his late thirties. I froze as our eyes locked. He glanced at the C train, then back at me, all while the angry man kept shouting in his ear.

"What are you waiting for?! Get him!"

The officer took a step in my direction—a long, loping, purposeful stride—followed quickly by another. He seemed larger than life, gliding across the concrete in his dark blue uniform, coming straight for me.

"You!" he said, and that's all I heard, because at that moment I did what any ten-year-old Black kid in New York would have done in that situation.

I ran.

Seven or eight quick steps across the platform, away from the cop and toward the front of the train, past the open doors and the nose of the car, until I stood at the edge of the platform, surrounded by a teeming mass of humanity. For an instant, I hesitated, until I heard, over my shoulder, the voice of the officer.

"Don't!"

And then I jumped.

It was a fall of less than four feet, from the platform onto the tracks, right in front of the train, which fortunately remained stationary, although not for much longer. In full view of what I can only presume was a horrified crowd of onlookers, I landed on my feet, hopped over the dreaded, electrified third rail, climbed up onto a narrow ledge, and proceeded to run through the tunnel, in the darkness, illuminated only by occasional exit signs. Desperate, frightened— of what, I can't say for sure, except that in my world, even at that age, the police were to be feared—I hustled through the tunnel, carefully placing one foot in front of the other, like a gymnast on a balance beam, scurrying along the ledge, which was intended only for the use of construction workers and other maintenance types, and certainly not for little boys on the run from law enforcement. I tried not to fall back onto the tracks, but even worse was the fear of a train coming by on the track nearest the ledge and pressing me up against the wall, so close that I'd feel the heat of its breath on my face.

What did I do? I wondered. *What do they want?*

Nearly paralyzed by fear, I leaned into a door beneath one of the exit signs. The door opened into more darkness, illuminated faintly by construction lights. Down a short hallway and into a small room, rising out of which was a steel ladder.

Up, I thought. *To the street. To freedom.* There was a steel hatch at the top of the ladder, thick and heavy. I leaned into it with my neck and shoulder, with every ounce of my spindly, ninety-pound frame. I punched the door. I yelled at it. It did not move an inch. It simply ignored me.

Terrified and exhausted, I retraced my steps, back out into the tunnel, and resumed running along the ledge, as trains sped by on the other side, moving in the opposite direction. Darkness gave way to light as I approached the next station. I could hear voices, the drone of a public address system announcing arrivals and departures, the screeching of wheels. I kept running along the ledge, certain now that I was going to be flattened by a train. I was so tired, so filthy, so scared that I barely noticed the figures approaching in the distance. They stopped on the ledge, waiting for me to come closer. I was much too frightened to turn around and go back, so I ran right to them, almost relieved to have the chase be done.

There were three officers. They guided me onto the tracks and then back up to the platform on the other side, where three more cops were waiting. I wonder how it must have looked—six uniformed officers from the New York Police Department forming a tight circle around one ten-year-old boy.

As I held up my hands in surrender and closed my eyes, I heard one of them say, "You're under arrest, kid." He turned me around, put my hands behind my back, and slapped a pair of handcuffs on me. Then, they dragged me away.

"What did I do?" I asked.

There was no answer.

"What did I do?" By now I was crying, spitting the words through tears and snot and sweat. "I'm sorry. I'm sorry."

They took me to the Seventy-Seventh Precinct, just off Utica Avenue, near Bergen Street, where I sat handcuffed to a pole, on a long bench with a half dozen other "criminals," the youngest of whom was old enough to be my father. If this sounds like a darkly comical scenario, well, it sure didn't feel that way. It was terrifying. Eventually, they led me into an interview room, handcuffed me to one of those straight-backed, brown wooden chairs, and proceeded to interrogate me. There were two of them now, both white, middle-aged.

"Just tell us you did it," one of the officers said.

"Did what?"

They looked at each other. One of them sighed. The other pursed his lips.

"You know what."

I shook my head. "No, sir. I don't."

"The robbery, boy. Just admit it. You robbed someone on the train. We know it was you—the victim identified you. Just tell us you did it, and you can go home."

"No," I said. "No . . . I didn't."

One of them rubbed his forehead in exasperation. I started to cry, softly at first and then openly—big, hacking sobs, so thick I could barely breathe.

"Why . . . are you . . . doing this?" I said, choking out the words between gasps for air. "I didn't steal anything."

I'd never felt so alone, powerless, scared. I look back on that moment now and think about how it continues to happen to Black kids to this day, nearly fifty years later. I understand how easily a confession can be coerced out of someone—particularly a young person—who has done nothing wrong; how in that moment, you might say anything just to get the hell out of the room and back home, and how that false confession could change the trajectory of your life. I understand how a group of innocent young boys could be transformed through intimidation and coercion into the Central Park Five.

But I didn't relent. I just sat there crying, saying the same thing, over and over. "I didn't do it."

That there was no evidence—no wallet with someone else's ID in my pocket, no cash—meant nothing. They presumed I had ditched whatever I had taken. What they had was an accusation: a white adult telling two white cops that he had been robbed by a Black kid.

A scared but stubborn little Black kid.

The cops got nicer as the proceeding dragged on.

"We know you're nervous," they said. "It's understandable. But everything will be okay if you just tell us you did it. You can go home."

By the time my mother arrived with my uncle Willie to pick me up, some five hours later, my throat was raw and my eyes bloodshot. It was as if I'd cried out a lifetime of fear all at once. This was the experience I'd been warned about. The threat we all felt as men in blue suits and shiny black shoes patrolled our streets, waiting for a slipup.

"What happened?" my mother asked

"I don't know. They think I stole something."

She gave me a hard look. "And . . . ?"

"I didn't do it. I didn't steal anything."

She nodded, looked at my uncle. It was his turn now.

"If something happened, Bruce, you need to tell us. Right now."

There was no bullshitting Uncle Willie. He was a tough guy, hard on his kids, kept them all on a short leash. An old-school parent, he was predisposed to believing that if you ended up in a police station, chances are you'd done something to deserve the visit.

I shook my head, started to cry again.

"I didn't do it. I swear."

He put a hand on my shoulder.

"It's okay. I believe you."

Eventually the cops led my mother and uncle out of the room. I sat alone for a while longer until they returned. The cops had explained to my mother that I would be allowed to leave but that they would be continuing their investigation and that they would be in touch.

As we walked out of the room, I could hear the cops talking to each other. I picked up snippets of the conversation, which they obviously weren't trying to hide.

"Ignorant niggers," I heard one of them say. I looked at my uncle, then at my mother. Neither said a word or betrayed an ounce of emotion. I don't know what they heard—if they heard anything at all. Maybe it hadn't surprised them. Maybe they knew this was not a place to try to wage a fair fight.

My mother took my hand in hers and squeezed it tight. I heard the sound of laughter as we walked away.

By the time we got back to my grandmother's house, it was close to midnight. When I walked in, she gave me a hug, told me to sit down at the kitchen table, and offered me something to eat. I was tired and filthy, the smell of petroleum from the subway tunnel rising off my clothes.

"I didn't do anything wrong, Grandmama," I said, even though she hadn't asked.

She smiled. "I know."

A week passed with no news from the police, no word on whether I'd be charged with some sort of crime or whether the mystery had been solved. I watched the day my frustrated mother pulled the officer's card she'd been handed at the precinct out of her purse and picked up the phone. She waited patiently while being put on hold repeatedly and transferred from one person to another. And I saw the expression of relief run across her face as she was finally told they had caught the kid who committed the robbery on the subway—the actual perpetrator! There was no apology, no acknowledgment of lives disrupted, or a young boy's innocence stolen. And I could tell by my mother's reaction that none was expected. She had the resigned look of a Black mother with no options but to send her son into the world with a wish for a better tomorrow. Her eyes, glassy with emotion, told a story: This is the world we live in. Better get used to it.

Chapter 3

THE HUSTLE

"**L**isten, Bruce, you're going to be repeating fourth grade next year."

That word: *repeating*. It sent a wildfire down my spine. I was only ten years old, but by that time every kid knows what it means to be held back, to be deemed a failure. To repeat is to *do over*, because you weren't smart enough to get it right the first time around. It is, to an elementary school kid, a pejorative of the highest order. Or maybe the lowest order.

"Repeating?" I said, almost choking on the word. "Why?"

"We all just think it would be better. It'll give you time to catch up."

Catch up. A phrase almost as degrading as *repeating*. These were words dripping with implication, and if my ten-year-old brain didn't quite understand the nuance of such a designation, it certainly understood the consequence. I was slow . . . stupid . . . lacking intellect and ambition. I was *less than*.

Education had played little more than a tangential role in my life until I moved to the Amsterdam Houses and enrolled in a school that was, interestingly enough, more middle class and ethnically diverse than the school I had attended in Brooklyn. I moved halfway through fourth grade; the following fall, when everyone else advanced to fifth grade, I was held back. I don't recall anyone sharing a specific reason for my reclassification—there was vague talk about having come from a weaker school and transferring halfway through the year—but I do remember that mixture of shame, anger, and helplessness.

The news was delivered in June, on the otherwise euphoric last day of school, students unable to sit still, teachers counting the minutes until the beginning of the blessed summer recess. When the final bell rang and everyone started for the door, my teacher, Mr. Stuart, asked me to stay behind for a moment. Like most of the faculty, he was middle-aged and white, but a rare male presence in one of the few professions (elementary school teacher) dominated by women. I remember him mostly as a benign figure, patient but disaffected. Now, though, he was serious, his tone solemn.

In the hallway, my friends and classmates were cleaning out cubbies and celebrating their release—the start of summer!—emboldened by the knowledge that they would be moving on. I walked glumly past them and out into the street, figuring I'd keep the secret to myself for as long as possible. I wondered, though, if they could sense what had happened, if the humiliation was now public, for it felt as though I had the word *dummy* stamped on my forehead.

When I got home, I tearfully broke the news to my mother. She was neither angry nor disappointed. Instead, she merely shrugged.

"Don't worry about it. You'll be okay."

"But, Mommy . . . they said I'm repeating."

She shook her head. "Doesn't matter."

And that was that. My mother's flat response—her lack of indignation or even empathy—was a reflection of the low value placed on education in an environment where day-to-day survival took precedence. Education wasn't looked down upon; it just wasn't looked at. Period. My mother was too busy raising kids and working and tending to some complicated health issues to lose sleep over whether her child had to repeat fourth grade. Was it really such a big deal? Apparently not.

"But all my friends are going on to fifth grade," I said.

"You'll make new friends."

"I just made new friends."

"Right, so you'll do it again."

"Mommy . . . am I stupid?"

She smiled. "No, it's just school. Doesn't mean anything."

She was wrong, of course, and I knew it; could feel it in my bones. There was absolutely no pressure on me at home to do well in school, to see education as a viable pathway to a better life. And why should there have been? You have to see the transformation—the opening of doors—to believe it, and my mother had as few role models, and as little personal experience in the matter, as me. School was simply what you did while waiting for the adult world to kick your ass. But on that day, when I walked out of PS 199, feeling like a failure, something changed. A judgment had been passed—a determination made by others who barely knew me—that I was inadequate when measured against my peers. And not from one of those outsiders deployed to corral and shame and police and confine. This came from people I'd grown to trust. It hurt, and I wanted to do whatever I could to avoid feeling that hurt again.

I wouldn't say this all took place overnight, at the age of ten, but I did understand on some level that if I worked harder, I would get better grades, and then these sorts of decisions would not be left to others. So, while it was painful, it was one of the most valuable lessons I ever learned.

My mother was right about one thing: I did make new friends, and I kept some of my old ones, as well. From a social standpoint, repeating fourth grade turned out to be less cataclysmic than I anticipated. For one thing, my new best friend was a boy named Freddie who lived in my building. Freddie was Puerto Rican; like me, he had an absentee father and, consequently, a rather long leash to do as he pleased. He was also a year younger than me, which meant we would now be classmates at PS 199. We spent a lot of time at each other's apartments, watching TV, eating each other's food, trying to figure out ways to keep busy.

In Manhattan, we had a newer, larger apartment, but the sense of community we had enjoyed in Brooklyn was no more. Gone were the tree-lined streets and the rows of brownstones populated by folks looking out for one another. We lived on top of each other at the Amsterdam Houses, a thousand families packed into roughly a dozen buildings, and the proximity sometimes had the paradoxical effect of creating distance and isolation. In Crown Heights, there were always kids playing in the streets, families sharing time and resources. Strange as it may sound to those unfamiliar with New York, you could breathe in Brooklyn.

Manhattan—or at least this corner of Manhattan—was different. It was, to my ten-year-old eyes, congested, loud, dangerous, impersonal.

Despite having a "nicer" place to live, we were still demonstrably poor. To stretch our budget, which was meager despite public assistance, we'd sometimes engage in activities that were not, strictly speaking, legal. For example, I would go to Alexander's department store with Freddie and another friend, Joe, and we'd change the stickers on items we needed— swapping the $1.99 tag on a pair of socks for the $3.99 on a shirt or a basketball. We didn't look at this as stealing (although obviously it was); it was a matter of obtaining that which we needed by paying whatever we could afford.

Discretionary income did not exist, so my siblings and I knew better than to ask for things that were not necessary. If we wanted something, we figured out how to get it. If we wanted a pet, we'd go to the Central Park children's zoo and steal something small—a chicken or a duck or whatever— and hide it under the sink at home until Mom found out and made us get rid of it. There was one time someone in the building gave us a dog. We were so happy and excited, until we realized the magnitude of the responsibility that came with it. There was plenty of love for the dog, but love doesn't fill the belly. Table scraps and garbage only went so far.

Eventually, we had to give the dog away because we couldn't afford to feed him.

Central Park functioned as our playground. We'd sneak onto the back of the horse-drawn carriages and hitch rides until we were shooed away. We'd take off our shoes and roll up our pants and jump into the water at Bethesda Fountain to retrieve coins that had been tossed away casually by tourists and wealthy Manhattanites. What was a quarter to them, invested foolishly in trying to make a wish come true? In our hands, at least, the money could be spent on food or clothing. It seemed a fair and reasonable exchange.

We stole not to be cruel or malevolent or out of some misplaced sense of adventure, or even to unleash our inner gangster (although, for some of us, that would come later). We stole because we lacked the things that so many other people took for granted.

I couldn't have been more than twelve or thirteen when we stole some fishing rods and tackle from Alexander's. Well, not stole, exactly. More like "underpaid." Freddie, Joe, and I, along with a couple other friends, played the price tag "game" with some cheaper items and the tags on the fishing gear. Then we hung out in the back of the store for a while, waiting for one of the female clerks to take over the cash register, because our preadolescent minds presumed a woman was less likely than a man to recognize that a fishing pole was supposed to cost more than three bucks. One could argue that we were trafficking in stereotypes, but we felt we were simply playing the odds, and it proved to be a solid bet. A short time later we walked out of the store, well equipped for a day of angling.

We didn't settle for tossing our lines into the dreary Hudson. Success there would have been unlikely, and the fish surely inedible anyway. Instead, we took the subway to Sheepshead Bay, Brooklyn, and paid for spots on a small fishing boat called the *Pilot 2*. For the next few hours, we cruised around the bay, hauling in bluefish by the bucketful. Back at the dock, the crew cleaned the fish for us and packed them in ice. We carried the bounty home, along with our gear, on a crowded subway train, feeling like we had conquered the world. There was nothing frivolous about our mission. We were young warriors, hunter-gatherers bringing home food for the family.

Necessity truly is the mother of invention, and I became industrious at a young age. No one was going to give me money to spend at the corner store, to go to the movies, to buy . . . well, anything. It simply didn't exist. So, I had to figure out a way to earn it. This could have gone a few different ways, most of them bad. I had friends who began selling drugs when they were barely in their teens, mostly marijuana, but also heroin, which was everywhere in the city during the early to mid-1970s, before cocaine came on the scene, and then crack after that. Some kids did it merely to earn money. Some also started using. I had friends who overdosed and died. I had other friends who got caught and arrested and quickly found themselves thrown into the vortex of the criminal justice system.

For a lot of kids—most of them, probably—there was no moral or ethical quandary about dealing drugs. They needed money, and this was the fastest way to get it. It was so common and pervasive that it didn't even seem like much of a risk. And yet, for some reason that I have never quite been able to pinpoint, I remained an observer rather than a participant. Fear, I suppose, was the primary motivation. I didn't want to die. I didn't want to go to jail. I didn't want to disappoint my mother and grandmother. I wanted something more out of life, and I had to figure out how to extract it.

My alternative to selling drugs was a job packing bags at a grocery store. I worked after school at a Chinese restaurant on Ninth Avenue, run by a man known to me only as Mr. Wu, chopping vegetables, steaming vats of rice, cleaning up around the kitchen. Whatever he needed. At the end of my shift, I'd get a few dollars and some containers of food to take home. For the longest time, I didn't understand why Mr. Wu had hired me—I was the only non Asian person working in the restaurant. At first, I figured he was just a nice guy trying to help me out. We had no formal arrangement you can't put a twelve-year-old on the payroll, after all. I had met him one day while walking home from school. I imagine he saw me every day, noticed the way I'd slow down as I passed, taking in the smell, wishing I had the money to pay for some chicken fried rice (or whatever). Eventually, he asked if I wanted a job. I said sure, and he handed me a broom and an apron.

"But first . . . you eat," he said, directing me to a small table in the back of the kitchen.

And that was the routine. I'd get an early dinner after school, work for a few hours, and then head home around eight or nine o'clock, armed with leftovers for the family (or friends who intercepted me before I entered the building) and a ten-dollar bill in my pocket; sometimes a twenty.

While I have no reason to believe that Mr. Wu was anything other than a generous man taking pity on a hungry kid from the neighborhood, I think it's fair to say that he was getting something out of the deal, as well. Mr. Wu, it turned out, figured if someone tried to rob his place, which was right next to the projects, I'd be able to identify them. Or maybe they'd hear that a Black kid from the neighborhood was working there and be less inclined to steal from a friendly proprietor or one of his delivery boys. Regardless, I guess you could say I was hired as a bit of twelve-year-old protection—if not exactly "muscle," at least an insurance policy.

My friends and I hustled. Running up to the line of taxis and other cars in front of Lincoln Center dropping off the rich folks for a night at the opera, opening the car doors and then waiting for someone to press a quarter or a dollar into our palms. No one asked us to do this, but no one stopped us, either. Or we would sneak into the New York Coliseum at Columbus Circle when there was an auto show or some other convention and pop open one of the back doors and offer half-price admission to anyone who might be interested.

At the end of these nights, which could stretch out for hours, we'd pool our resources—like servers and busboys at a restaurant sharing tips—and go out for pizza or burgers, sitting together in the park, or in front of the Manhattan campus of Fordham University, home to the school's graduate division and law school. I knew nothing about Fordham—or college in general—other than that the campus was bright and beautiful. Like Lincoln Center, of which it was a neighbor, Fordham's campus was clean and well-groomed in a way that reflected nothing so much as wealth and privilege. And eating fast food on the sidewalk outside one of the administrative buildings was as close to that world as any of us was ever likely to get.

Our most lucrative and reliable source of income came from the newspaper industry. The scheme was the brainchild of my buddy Joe. We were walking by a newsstand one morning before school and spotted an unopened bundle of newspapers. The owner was still setting up for the day and had yet to organize his stock, even as customers began to swarm his stand.

Joe slowed down as we walked by, kept eyeing the bundle of newspapers.

"I got an idea," he said.

And so our little bootlegging operation was born. We recruited Freddie and a few others and quickly went to work. We'd get up at five in the morning and hang out near one of the many newsstands or kiosks that dotted the borough, waiting for a delivery truck to drop off a bundle. It was astoundingly easy: all you had to do was show up before the owner of the newsstand arrived, cut open the package, and walk off with a hundred copies of the *Daily News* or *New York Post*. Then, you could hawk them to passersby on any corner for fifty cents on the dollar. Even better, we could take them back to the projects and sell them door-to-door, half price.

After a while, I branched out, hired a few of my friends from Brooklyn to come up on Sundays and help with distribution. We "borrowed" grocery carts from a supermarket to collect the papers, then we'd bring them back to the Amsterdam Houses to break up the bundles and sort them into manageable packs. By the time I was thirteen, I had put away enough to buy my own little color television set, a thirteen-inch Panasonic that I kept in my bedroom. (Freddie bought a JVC boom box that he'd carry with him practically everywhere, like Radio Raheem, blasting music for the entire neighborhood.) Needless to say, we did not have a color TV in our house; in fact, I didn't know anyone who had a color TV. But now I had one. In my bedroom. It was mine and mine alone, the fruit of ingenuity and hard labor.

"Where did that come from?" my mother asked one day.

"Selling papers," I said.

"Mmmm-hmmm."

I mean, it wasn't *not* true. My mother knew I was selling newspapers; she just didn't know about the stealing part of the operation. Frankly, she had neither the time nor the inclination to investigate the matter further. I was working; I was making money; I was staying out of jail and away from drugs. In her mind, I suppose, it could have been a whole lot worse.

My father had a different take on things. He came back into our lives a little bit when we moved to the projects, for reasons that were never made clear. Suddenly, there he was again, this man I barely knew, saying he was my father, trying to exert influence and order without having put in the groundwork. He could be abrasive, overbearing, and I resented him suddenly assuming the role of parent based strictly on biological history. But he was not without attributes. My dad was a smart but volatile man who would implore me to read a book and "turn off the damn ignorant box" if I was parked in front of the TV for too long (which in his mind was the moment the screen lit up). He made sure we all did chores around the house, and if there was nothing to do, he'd come up with something. He was a follower of Malcolm X (he was even present the night Malcolm was assassinated at the Audubon Ballroom in Washington Heights) who liked to talk about race and philosophy. Sometimes he'd recite one of his favorite poems, Jackie Earley's "One Thousand Nine Hundred and Sixty-Eight Winters":

> *Got up this morning*
> *Feeling good and black*
> *Thinking black thoughts*
> *Did black things*
> *Played all my black records*
> *And minded my own black bidness*
> *Put on my best black clothes*
> *Walked out my black door*
> *And, Lawd have mercy*
> *White Snow!*

I didn't understand this poem at the time, but I get it now. You can live a Black life at home, in your own bubble, but when you walk out the door it's a white world. That's what my father wanted us to realize. In a lot of ways, he was a conscious fellow, but to a twelve- or thirteen-year-old kid hustling to make a few bucks so he could buy clothes for the new school year and not look like the rattiest kid in class, he was mainly just an annoyance.

My father had been suspicious about the sudden influx of money that supposedly resulted from "selling newspapers."

Unlike my mother, he was unwilling to turn a blind eye. Instead, unbeknownst to me, my father invested considerable time and effort into busting our burgeoning operation. He rose early, shortly after I left the house, and followed me and my buddies as we ran around town, gathering up bundles of stolen newspapers. And when he discovered that my little operation was very much out of the gangster bootlegging playbook, he came down hard.

"You keep stealing shit," he said, "I'll call the cops."

"What are you talking about? I'm not stealing anything."

In that moment, I realized how pathetically unconvincing I sounded. It had only been a couple years since I had sturdily professed my innocence to a bunch of NYPD cops who had accused me of theft on a subway train. This was different. Now I really was a thief, and a liar, as well. It felt awful. My father had a finely tuned bullshit detector, having been something of a bullshitter in his own right. The fact that I did not immediately acknowledge my misdeeds further stoked his anger. Stealing was bad enough; treating him like a fool was worse.

"I followed you, son," he said, shaking his head in disgust. "I saw what you did. I watched you and your boys. And I'm telling you now, this shit is over. You keep it up, I'll hand all of you over to the cops myself."

I didn't say a word, just stared at him, simultaneously impressed that he had managed to track us without being noticed and angry that he thought he now had the right to tell me what to do, after so much time away.

"You think I'm bluffing?"

I held his gaze, then finally withered and turned away.

"No, sir."

Whatever flaws my father might have had—and there were many, mostly stemming from his own wildly dysfunctional childhood—he was wise to recognize the slippery slope that connects low-level teenage street hustling to grown-up crime and prison. What he failed to recognize (more likely, he didn't care) is that he wasn't just messing with my money; he was messing with my friends' money, and they were none too happy about it.

"We should take him out, man," one of my buddies suggested, after I told them we were going to have to shut down the business.

"Take him out?" I repeated, as if there was some question as to what he meant.

"Yeah, why not? What's he to you, anyway?"

"Well . . . he's my father."

"Nah . . ."

Thankfully, that plan never went beyond the talk stage, but we were getting old enough that real crime—violent or otherwise—was a persistent presence in our lives. Even in middle school, I saw friends of mine carrying stacks of cash bigger than we got for selling newspapers. Some of it was drug money. Some of it came from mugging clueless tourists and Upper West Siders wandering near Lincoln Center, unaware that rougher neighborhoods were just across the street.

But I also saw kids getting arrested and going away, not just for days or weeks, but for months on end. One day we'd be playing basketball together, and the next day they'd be gone. More than a few ended up at the notorious Spofford Juvenile Detention Center in the Bronx, one of a subset of New York jails described in 1984 by the Supreme Court as "indistinguishable from a prison." And yet, the clientele at Spofford was exclusively adolescent, with an entire inmate population made up of children no more than fifteen years of age. It was, in every sense of the phrase, a prison for boys, which made it ripe for all manner of human rights violations and abuses, some perpetrated by corrections officers, and some by the inmates themselves. I knew kids who returned from stints at Spofford damaged if not broken, with stories of roach-infested dining halls and rats crawling across their beds at night; of beatings and sexual abuse and suicide.

Some pretended not to be affected by the experience, or to have found it a rite of passage. But I could see in their eyes that this wasn't true. I could see what it had done to them.

I saw kids committing grown-up crimes and doing grown-up time. I saw children getting shot and killed. Guns were now far more prevalent, easily accessible to the aspiring middle school gangbanger or drug dealer. And I began to reconsider. Maybe the money wasn't so easy, after all. Maybe it was just *quick* money.

Chapter 4

JUST TRY. ONCE.

I wasn't the best-looking kid in the projects, nor the best athlete. And I didn't walk around with wads of drug money. But I knew how to talk. I was fifteen when I first made a friend I'd call a girlfriend. Sonia was pretty, and our relationship advanced quickly; she was my first in all the ways you'd imagine at that age. But a cloud hung over my head the entire time we were together. The teenage moms in the neighborhood, absentee dads, the desperate breadwinners committing crimes to help pay for their kids . . . it looked like a trap. So, I ran.

Idle hands and idle minds. The devil's playground. All that Pentecostal stuff that sounds silly to a little kid but, as I'd learn, is rooted in truth.

Just stay busy. Keep moving . . . moving . . . moving.

My first refuge was basketball. You could fill a day on any of a dozen nearby courts, playing long and hard, until you were totally drained of anger and frustration. I wouldn't be going pro anytime soon, but with all the trouble I could get into in the neighborhood, shooting hoops was a welcome respite to those looking over me. Aunt Viola appreciated almost any distraction that wasn't running drugs or fighting on the block, but she always had her mind on something more. My cousins Phillip and LaTasha, her kids, had been nudged into performing arts. A tough road, for sure, but a little more likely to translate into a scholarship or job than what I'd been doing. Aunt Viola found subsidized programs in the arts, paid for lessons when the city didn't pick up the tab, and shepherded her kids from one venue to another.

"Why don't you tag along," she told me one day. "Maybe you'll like it."

"Uhhhh, I don't know . . ."

"Just try. Once."

Phillip dreamed of being an R&B singer, and LaTasha was an aspiring ballerina. Unlike my mother, Aunt Viola believed in the power of education—in all its myriad forms—and wanted to expose her kids to as many opportunities as possible. Time spent onstage or in a dance studio, she reasonably figured, was time that couldn't be spent on the street. Her kids would learn self-discipline. They would be well-rounded. They would be safe. More than most of the adults I knew, Aunt Viola had it all figured out.

I was blessed to be in her orbit.

Nevertheless, I was at first a reluctant student of the arts. It just wasn't the sort of thing the boys I hung around did—dancing, singing, acting—and I couldn't imagine the abuse I would face if any of my friends found out I was even entertaining such a notion. I was a street kid. A hustler. A tough guy in the making.

But a funny thing happened when we arrived at the dance studio to pick up LaTasha. I saw all the pretty girls in their leggings and skirts and immediately reconsidered. I didn't have a lot of talent as a dancer—actually, I didn't have any talent—but one thing I could do was memorize lines and parrot them back out. I could *act*. Like, legitimately. Who knew?!

With Aunt Viola's support—she paid the six-dollar weekly fee—I enrolled in an acting class at a private school in Brooklyn. The first few months were devoted to learning basic technique, role-playing exercises, acting out short scenes from well-known plays; there was vocal training, as well. Then, we began rehearsing for a year-end play that would be staged by all the students in the school.

I enjoyed everything about my introduction to theater. I found the stage liberating in a way that I had not anticipated. I liked to transport myself somewhere else. I was never the class clown or the first person to volunteer to read an assignment out loud. I was just . . . there. Taking up space, minding my business. Flying below the radar. The idea of standing on a stage, with a spotlight on my face, delivering lines that I had spent months committing to memory, with the very real possibility of failure and embarrassment at stake—well, that did not exactly fit my established notion of fun. How odd, then, to be completely transfixed by the experience and to crave more of it.

I stayed in the Brooklyn program throughout middle school, devoting increasing amounts of time and energy. Along the way, I caught the eye of an agent—a woman who had seen me in one of the year-end productions and reached out to our program director. In retrospect, this process—of hitting the local theater groups and high schools on the off chance one of the dozens of young performers that night shows "it," whatever "it" may be—sounds like a brutal way to make a living; and, perhaps, a little exploitative of the kids practicing their crafts, but at the time, I was just thrilled that an agent saw something in me that I wasn't sure existed.

"You have talent," she said that day in her Midtown office. "But you need to branch out. The kids who make it on Broadway, they're what we like to call 'triple threats.'" She paused. "Do you know what that is, Bruce, a triple threat?"

I shook my head. "No, ma'am."

"A triple threat is someone who is more than just an actor. They can sing and dance."

I nodded. That made sense.

"And because they can sing and dance, as well as act, they have more opportunities to work. Do you understand?"

"Yes, ma'am."

She smiled. "Good. I think you have a future in this business."

I suppose it's possible that I was, to her, just another line in the water—an eager kid with a modicum of ability who might, with enough training and luck and ambition, evolve into a revenue stream. A professional actor from whom she would extract a 10 percent commission on every paying gig. It didn't matter. All I heard was "You have talent." And that was enough to keep me going.

In high school I began taking instruction at the Frederick Douglass Creative Arts Center in Manhattan, which offered seminars, workshops, and school programs for aspiring African American artists, performers, and writers. It was there that I discovered just how ferocious the competition would be for all of us who hoped to one day be worthy of the term *professional actor*. And that, in fact, was only one of my goals. I wanted to become not just a working actor but a *star*! To be honest, I was chasing fame (and the accoutrements that presumably went along with it) as much as anything else. I wanted to be a good actor, but I was less interested in the art form than in gaining access to a world that otherwise seemed unattainable. A world of cars and money and mansions, of swimming pools and beautiful girls. I wanted to be loved and admired and respected.

I was, to put it mildly, a bit naive.

For the next few years, almost until high school graduation, I lived a secret life centered around musical theater acting. And almost all of it was free and sponsored by the city of New York. At Frederick Douglass, I took instruction in both drama and musicals. Another program at John Jay College was oriented toward film and television, led by a woman who had significant experience working as an actress on "daytime dramas" (soap operas, as they were commonly known). Many of the soaps were filmed in New York, so her presence brought a degree of realism to the proceedings—*she's done this; she's a legitimate actor!*

These were, I quickly discovered, entirely different types of creative endeavors. Onstage, we were taught to be big—to project to the back of the room. To use all our physical and creative power to rise above the stage and be seen and heard. On film and television, everyone is larger than life. The objective, then, was to be small, understated. Onstage, in a live performance, you had to smile with the zeal of a ventriloquist's dummy in order to be seen and understood by the audience. If you did that on camera, you'd ridiculous. Onstage, every movement was exaggerated and pronounced. On camera, you had to rein yourself in so that you didn't overwhelm the story or the actors around you. In some ways, they were diametrically opposed approaches to the same craft.

At John Jay, I took classes in ethnic dance, along with vocal lessons that taxed both my patience and ability. *Do-re-mi* . . . *Do-re-mi* . . . over and over, up and down the scales, until my throat burned and I was bored out of my mind.

"Can't we just sing the songs?" I'd ask.

The teacher would respond with a mix of disdain and pity.

"You must walk before you can run, Mr. Jackson."

"Huh?"

"If you don't master the scales, you will never be a true singer. You will be a fraud."

Other students joined the class and advanced beyond scales with ease. They would move on to real singing, while I was stuck on *do-re-mi*. I got the point. And while I might have been an adequate basketball player, I lacked the grace and athleticism to be a competent dancer. Try as I might, I was never going to be even a double threat, let alone triple.

But I stuck with it, figuring there was always room for an unspectacular talent who reliably hit his marks. In high school, I even got to perform in a Lincoln Center production of *Runaways*, a popular Broadway musical about street kids in New York. I had only a few lines and didn't have to do any singing or dancing, but the experience was still a trip. Just a few years earlier I had been opening car doors for a quarter in front of Lincoln Center, wondering what it looked like inside, and now here I was onstage!

Even as I rose up the ranks a bit, I still expended a lot of energy hiding my love for theater from my friends. I lived a double life—playing basketball and partying and hanging out with my buddies in the projects all day during the week . . . and then sneaking off for rehearsal or vocal lessons on the weekends or in the evenings. If my guys Freddie or Joe wanted to hang out but I had to be at John Jay for a class or rehearsal, I'd just make up an excuse.

"Sorry, man. Going to Grandmama's house."

"Okay, later."

There were times when the secrecy weighed on me, when I wanted to share my dreams with one of my buddies, but I never did. In my entire circle of friends, there wasn't a single actor, dancer, or singer. I didn't want to be different . . . strange. A *weirdo*. I wanted to fit in. So I toggled quietly, surreptitiously between worlds.

For several years, I clung to the dream of trying to make a career out of acting. Thanks to my agent, I even auditioned for a role on the daytime drama *All My Children*. Didn't get it, which is probably for the best, but it wouldn't be my last dance with the entertainment industry.

Martin Luther King Jr. High School in Manhattan was a whole different vibe for me. Kids walking around in designer jeans and jackets, and clean white sneakers that left me full of envy. Many of these kids were from Harlem and were just as poor as I was, but they had made *decisions* that provided them with quite a bit more than I had.

Easy money. The way of life that kept my neighborhood chock-full of pills and heroin, cocaine and weed—all on demand, all the way back to when I was twelve or thirteen.

I grew frustrated, thought about joining their ranks, but figured if I was going to dabble in more serious criminal activity—primarily drug dealing or theft—it would be safer to get something started back in Brooklyn than it would be in Harlem. And by "safer," I don't mean less likely to be arrested, but rather, less likely to be stabbed or shot. Uptown was rough, no way around it, and while I might have tried at times to evince the character of a gangster, I was never much more than a poseur. Kids started going away again, disappearing for a few weeks at a time, or a few months, returning with those horrific tales of Spofford. Fear, healthy and strong, got the best of me. Every time I was tempted to walk on the wild side, something would happen—often something terrible— that illustrated in graphic terms the punishing permanence of our choices. I never did sell drugs, never robbed or assaulted anyone. Never owned a gun or even a knife. I flew between the shadows and the light to get by without too much trouble.

One weekend when I was fifteen, I visited Phillip at his home in the Brownsville section of Brooklyn—farther out east than my old home in Crown Heights. Although Aunt Viola kept a tidy place in the projects, there was no denying that Brownsville was a rough neighborhood. Shootings at least a couple times a week, omnipresent gangs, and a heavy drug trade. One of Phillip's best friends, Troy, was the same age as me. He was a nice-enough kid, and we spent a fair amount of time together, hanging out, playing basketball, listening to music. But by this time, Troy had already graduated from selling dime bags of weed to occasionally trafficking in heroin and other narcotics. We tried to dissuade him, but he'd always cut the lecture short.

"You've got options," he'd say to me. "I don't. This is all I've got."

This was not true. Troy was smart, ambitious, charismatic—those attributes, channeled in another way, could have carried him to a completely different life. But as a young man, he really believed there was no other way out. And I don't question his assumption, either. Therein lies the tragedy—Troy didn't have anyone in his life who could point him in another direction, the way my mother and grandmother and Aunt Viola did; or threaten him with real consequences, the way my father had done. At fifteen, it was already too late. The money from dealing dope becomes as addictive as the substance itself. And leaves stains perhaps too hard to ever fully wash away unless you get out of the neighborhood entirely. Troy was making more money than most grown men in the neighborhood. He knew the risks but seemed to accept them as merely the price of doing business.

"I've got it under control. Don't worry."

Phillip, Aunt Viola's pride and joy, both benefited from and chafed under her firm rule. She was careful about letting her children run loose in the city—kids are kids, and by the time they are in their teens, they are determined to find their own way in the world. I have no doubt that Aunt Viola suspected that Troy was involved in some dangerous, illegal activity. At the same time, he was a sweet and polite kid— "Hi, Mrs. Jackson, I'm going to the store. Can I get anything for you while I'm there?"—who could walk around Browns- ville mostly unbothered, for he had, as they say, a reputation. In that way, he represented a kind of compromise for the family. Somewhat of a "man on the inside" to shield Aunt Viola's kids from the worst of the worst. He had clients. He had business partners. He had friends. And he also had enemies. On balance, though, Troy's company was valuable. If we wanted to leave the house and walk around the neighborhood, we would call Troy and see if he wanted to join us. I can only imagine the conflicting emotions this must have provoked in my aunt—the notion that we were safer in the company of a drug dealer. But that's the way it was. Until it wasn't.

One day, shortly after I arrived, the three of us spent a couple hours in front of Aunt Viola's apartment, holding court on a bench in front of the building. We tried to strike up conversations with girls as they passed by, but I noticed that something seemed off with Troy. He had the busy-eyed demeanor of someone whose attention was elsewhere. After a while, another kid walked by, a few years older. As he approached, Troy subtly opened his jacket to reveal a handgun. The other kid nodded, kept going. A few minutes later, he returned.

"What's up?" Troy asked.

"It's getting hot," the kid responded. Then he looked at Phillip and me. "You guys should go."

Phillip and I each looked at Troy. He nodded. "Get out of here."

We knew better than to argue, or to try to talk Troy into leaving with us. We hurried into the building and began climbing the stairs to Phillip's apartment. We were still in the stairwell when I heard the shots. Not a single *blam!*, but a rapid burst of fire. *Pop-pop-pop-pop!* If you'd never spent any time in a place like Brownsville, you might hear something like that and mistake it for fireworks. But by then, I knew the difference. We spilled into the apartment to find

Aunt Viola at the window, a look of panic on her face. And then relief.

"I thought it was you," she said, as we ran to join her.

I looked out, tentatively, at first, fearful of the possibility that at any moment a stray bullet might scream into Aunt Viola's living room. But I couldn't look away. There was Troy, slumped over on the bench. His friend was on the ground next to him. Blood splattered all over the bench and sidewalk. People gathered around, shouting and running. Within seconds, the sound of sirens filled the air.

The cops showed up and taped off the scene, conducting interviews and taking photographs around the motionless, bloody, untouched bodies of Troy and his nameless friend. An ambulance did show up eventually, but with no one left alive to treat, the bodies were covered with white sheets to await transport to the city morgue. If you survive a shooting, you go to the hospital right away. But if you don't, well, what's the rush? Troy's corpse sat there in the open for what felt like hours. Not a single police officer came to Aunt Viola's door to ask if we had seen anything, or if we had any connection to the deceased. You might think that the cops would canvass the building, interview all potential witnesses. But that did not happen. In the projects, no one ever sees anything. You keep your head down and your mouth shut. No one knows that better than the cops. It's just another murder—Black folks killing Black folks. Happens all the time, right? Who cares?

At one point, a woman arrived. She tried to break through the lines of yellow tape, crying and screaming, but the police held her back. I later found out that this was Troy's mother.

Aunt Viola watched her writhing, wailing, and shook her head in despair.

"Not right to bury your child," she said. Then, she paused. "What happened?"

Phillip and I exchanged glances. We both shrugged, said nothing.

"You're lucky," Aunt Viola said. "God was with you today."

In the days leading up to Troy's funeral, there was considerable talk in the neighborhood of conspiracies and retribution; the possibility that whoever had killed Troy and his friend might show up at the service, determined to turn a peaceful, respectful community event into a bloodbath. Thankfully, that proved to be nothing more than melodrama. It seemed unreal to me, the idea that a kid my age—a friend—had been shot and killed just moments after we had been talking. And now friends, relatives, and clergy gathered around to commemorate another case of what could have been. Troy was a popular kid. A smart kid. I knew that dealing drugs was dangerous, but more in the sense of legal ramifications—you sell enough shit, eventually the cops will catch you and you'll go to jail. This was different. This was glaring evidence that certain behaviors, not uncommon among my peer group, could also get you killed.

More than anything else from that funeral, I remember the sight of Troy's mother, crying hysterically, endlessly, the grief rising from some unimaginable depth. It wasn't just violence and death that I feared. It was the aftermath—the impact on those I loved and those who loved me. I remember thinking, *I don't want my mom to go through this. I don't want that to be me.*

Chapter 5

THE WORLD OUTSIDE MY DOOR

It sounded like such a good idea at the time.

I had just started tenth grade at Martin Luther King Jr. High School, where I was invited to participate in a co-op program combining school with practical workplace experience. I'd go to school one week, and then the next week I'd go to my job working in the printing room in the basement of Chase Manhattan Bank on Water Street in Lower Manhattan. But it turned out to be less of an opportunity than the implementation of a ceiling on goals and aspirations. Sure, the co-op kept me busy and put some money in my pocket, but it was basically a trade program designed to funnel kids into the workforce right after high school, and in the process, it usually diverted them from any hope of higher education. When I told my mother that I had entered the co-op program, she was happy, proud; her boy was becoming a man, taking care of business, earning his own way.

That I might also be forfeiting the possibility of becoming the first person in my family to attend college, and thus break a cycle of poverty, simply didn't factor into the equation. I was young, poor, short-sighted, and impulsive. And there was no one around to point any of this out, to explain the ramifications of my decision. I was a kid from the projects choosing to make money in an honest and acceptable manner. What could possibly be wrong with that? That I hated the job didn't matter in the least. I figured a job was something you were supposed to hate—isn't that why they called it *work*? It wasn't so much that the job was physically demanding— aside from the fact that we were on our feet all day, there was nothing physical about it. It was the crushing boredom that made it unbearable, the sameness of the work, day after dreary day.

On co-op days (weeks), I would rise early, have some breakfast, and then take the subway downtown to 1 Chase Plaza, a sprawling corporate complex employing thousands of workers at every level of global commerce, from seven-figure executives to the lowliest of clerical drones. Appropriately enough, we toiled in the basement, scarcely exposed to natural light or air, making copies of pamphlets, books, corporate reports—whatever needed replicating. I would spend the entire day, eight hours straight, standing at a copier, hypnotized by the endless collating of pages and the incessant hum of the machine. It never slept, never rested, merely paused once in a while to be cleaned or reloaded with ink. Then, I'd box the pages and place them in a cavernous mail slot to be delivered somewhere within the labyrinthine halls of Chase Plaza.

Once in a while, if we were short of delivery personnel, or if someone couldn't come down to the basement to pick up their copies, I'd get a chance to deliver them myself. After a while, I began to pray for these opportunities, for they offered a respite from the stench of toner and other chemicals and the headaches they could induce. Like mole people we'd emerge from the basement squinting and coughing, at once recoiling from the sun streaking through windows and basking in its warmth and its implication of freedom.

The biggest copiers, cranking out a hundred pages a minute, were always operated by the old-timers—a racially diverse mix of men (almost all of them were male) in their forties and fifties, with decades of experience. They were uniformly grim, going about their business with bleak stoicism. Most of them were practically mute; those who did engage in conversation were either darkly humorous, or merely dark.

"How long you been here, kid?"

"Three months."

"Hah! Thirty more years and you can start thinking about retirement! 'Course, they'll be doing all this with robots by then, probably."

I laughed, but the truth was, the idea of spending my life in the bowels of Chase Plaza was terrifying. I didn't know what I wanted to do, but I sure as hell didn't want to end up like these guys—miserable, regretful, lonely. Old men at forty.

What I failed to recognize was the ease with which a life's trajectory can be shaped by seemingly unimportant decisions; how hard it is to change direction once you are on a certain path. I was a few months into the co-op program when my history teacher, Mr. Lavin, pulled me aside one day after class and asked if I had given any thought to life after high school.

I shrugged. "Some. A little, maybe."

At this point, I was still deeply involved in theater and hoping to perhaps find a career in show business, but that wasn't something I was even willing to share with my friends. I certainly wasn't going to tell my history teacher. So, I told him what I presumed he wanted to hear.

"I guess I'll go to college."

He stared at me blankly, so I gave him a little more.

"I've always kind of wanted to be a lawyer. That would be cool, huh?"

This was not entirely a lie. I had watched *Perry Mason* reruns as a kid and thought that being a lawyer—the kind who spent half his time in the courtroom, and the other half playing private detective, neatly and quickly solving high-profile murder cases that in real life would drag on for months or years—seemed like a pretty good gig. But by the look on Mr. Lavin's face, I could tell he did not exactly see me as the next Perry Mason.

"Bruce," he finally said. "Let's be honest. You're not really college material . . . are you?"

There was a pause of indeterminant length. I found myself almost light-headed at the cavalier way in which he had dispensed this judgment, as if it wouldn't bother me, as if it were the most obvious thing in the world.

"Are you?"

I did not respond but simply picked up my books and walked out of the room.

I'd like to say this was a pivotal, sobering moment in my life—and it was, to some degree. The thing about change is that it rarely occurs overnight, especially as an adolescent. I did in fact begin to put more effort into my academic work, but I was unwilling to withdraw from the co-op program, which, despite its unrelenting tedium and obvious distraction from school, nevertheless provided the sort of income and security I wanted. In retrospect, I can say with complete confidence that the co-op program, while not the best choice for a college-bound student, proved valuable in many ways, not least because it taught me two things: (1) the importance of showing up every day and doing a job to the best of your ability, even when you dislike the job; (2) I was more ambitious than I wanted to admit.

Sometimes the best thing about a lousy part-time job is that it makes you realize what you don't want out of life, which can be almost as important as figuring out what you do want. I didn't know whether I wanted to be the next Sidney Poitier or the next Perry Mason, but I sure as hell knew I didn't want to be that guy in the basement of Chase Plaza, hunched over, coughing, beaten to a pulp by twenty-five years at the copier.

Something else I knew: I didn't want to go to jail, or get beaten or shot, things that seemed to be happening with increasing regularity among my friends.

My mother saw the writing on the wall, realized that no amount of basketball or acting lessons or even eight-hour shifts at Chase could shield me from the reality of life in the projects. So, one night, while we talked with an unusual degree of transparency about my fears, she offered a suggestion.

"You know, if you want, you could go live with your grandmother for a while."

Startled, I didn't say anything at first. It was almost like she had been reading my mind.

"It's quiet there," my mother said. "Peaceful. You'll get more work done."

I nodded. "Maybe, yeah."

Looking back, I would probably consider this to be a lateral move in terms of safety and bad influences, but it was a pivotal decision born of desperation and love—a change of scenery that wasn't really much of a change at all. I had friends in Brooklyn, both in Crown Heights, where I had grown up and where my grandmother still lived, and in East New York, where some of my cousins lived. There was crime and violence in Brooklyn—the murder of my friend Troy being the most obvious example—just as there was at the Amsterdam Houses. But at least I wouldn't be entrenched in any sort of a crew. And my grandmother had more time to keep an eye on me than my mother did.

As for the part about it being more peaceful? Well, that wasn't quite accurate. Grandmama welcomed me despite the fact that her one-bedroom apartment was already crowded— Phillip and LaTasha were frequent guests, as was another of my cousins, Ernestine, and Aunt Viola. And my mother. Grandmama opened her home to everyone, never complained about a lack of space. On many nights there would be five of us in that one bedroom, sharing three beds. If that was my mother's idea of peaceful or quiet, well, I didn't see it. Still, it was worth a try.

The next day, I packed a duffel bag with my meager belongings and moved back to Brooklyn, though I remained a student at Martin Luther King Jr. High School. Officially, nothing changed. Practically speaking, a great deal changed. For one thing, the days grew longer, busier, more complicated.

Grandmama would always rise first, around 5:00 a.m. She'd get the paper, make coffee, then wake me up around six. By six thirty, I was out of the house, walking to the subway station. Two trains and fifty-five minutes later, I'd be in Manhattan, walking to MLK. The total commute, including time walking to and from subway stations, was close to an hour and a half.

On school days, this was the schedule, morning and night. It was exhausting, but I got used to the routine, and the constant movement. Additionally, there were play rehearsals and vocal lessons. Most nights, I'd stagger back to my grandmother's house, so tired I could barely keep my eyes open. Although conflicting schedules made family dinners a rare thing, I never went hungry. Grandmama would always make a big meal and leave it on the stove or in the fridge for everyone to eat at their convenience. I woke often to the smell of grits with sardines and tomato sauce, a pungent and inexpensive breakfast staple. Chicken with red rice was a dinner favorite. And pound cake, sweet and dense, almost every day.

In the evening, whenever I did get around to eating, my grandmother would hang out in the kitchen and talk with me, ask how my day went. We played board games to pass the time. Grandmama's favorite was a game called Trouble, an uncomplicated game in which the object for each player was to send four game pieces around a board. The gimmick of Trouble was a plastic bubble—hemispherical in shape and glued to the center of the board—that contained two dice. Rather than rolling the dice, each player would press the "pop-o-matic" bubble, which would give off a sharp crackle as the dice ricocheted off the plastic dome and then settled on the surface of the board. It would have been easier to just toss

71

the dice, like every other board game, but the pop-o-matic bubble added a layer of silliness and fun.

There were only a few rules governing the world of Trouble, the most serious of which was: if you landed on a spot occupied by an opponent's piece, you could send that piece all the way back to the starting line. You were not, however, allowed to touch the opponent's game piece with your hand; he had to move it himself. I violated this rule with alarming frequency. I'd not just remove the piece but toss it off the board in mock triumph, a gesture that brought out the competitive spirit in my grandmother.

"Dammit, boy! Don't you do that again!"

"Sorry, Grandmama."

And then we'd laugh.

Those are the moments I remember, the ones that seem so inconsequential—a family sitting around the kitchen table, playing a silly board game, laughing and teasing each other. I was fifteen years old—an age when many of my friends and classmates would not have been caught dead playing games with their grandparents or siblings or cousins. Or maybe they just didn't have the opportunity. I did. And while I may not have realized it then, I was lucky. Granted, I was poor, and I did not have a father consistently present in my life. But I had family. I had people who worried about me and who held me accountable. People whose lives would have been altered if I suddenly screwed up or disappeared. I had support and guidance (just not the academic kind).

I had love.

We were not a squeaky-clean clan. Black Sam might have been an extreme example, but he was not the only person in our extended family who dabbled in criminal activity. There were family members who sold drugs, cousins who ran with gangs. Most of them passed through Grandmama's house at one time or another. We blended seamlessly together, the lawbreakers and the law abiders, each quietly respecting, or at least tolerating, the other's choices. We were connected by blood and history, at the nexus of which was my grandmother, staunch and maternal and welcoming.

As I grew from childhood into adolescence, I found it increasingly difficult to separate the good guys from the bad. The lines between right and wrong were not just blurred but washed away entirely. Given the choice, I trusted my cousins who ran with gangs more than I did anyone in law enforcement. The world outside my door was not safe, but not always for the reasons you might think.

To me, the murder of George Floyd at the hands of Minneapolis police officers in the summer of 2020 was shocking not necessarily because it happened but because of the public response—the collective national outrage over an act of police brutality all too commonly seen and ignored in the Black community. But it's important to remember that his death, tragically, was not unique; he was merely the latest and loudest example. If you're Black, chances are you have been impacted by a George Floyd moment. You may even have witnessed one yourself.

I was fifteen years old when I saw the tail end of a well-publicized incident in which the NYPD killed a thirty-year-old Black man in Crown Heights. Arthur Miller had immigrated to the United States from the Bahamas with his family as a teenager. By the summer of 1978, he had become a prominent local businessman whose various interests included a grocery store on Nostrand Avenue. He also was a community activist who had helped form a trained neighborhood watch group called the Four Block Association. He wanted the residents of his neighborhood to feel safe, both from criminals and from the police officers who sometimes harassed and abused the locals.

On a simpler level, Arthur was a nice guy who would hire neighborhood kids, like me—when I was younger, and before I moved to Manhattan—to do small chores: taking out trash behind a building he managed, sweeping sidewalks in front of his store. Easy stuff that he could have done himself, and that didn't take much time, but that he handed off because he wanted us to feel useful and have a few bucks in our pockets. It was Arthur's nature to get involved. To be concerned. To be a righteous citizen. In the end, that's what got him killed.

It began with a traffic stop involving Arthur's brother, Sam Miller, who was driving one of Arthur's trucks. According to the official NYPD report on the incident, Sam had been stopped so that police could serve a previous violation for littering. That led to the revelation that he was driving with a suspended license, which in turn led to an encounter of escalating and public volatility, during which Arthur Miller was called to the scene to help his brother. What followed was an intense and violent encounter involving the two brothers and more than a dozen police officers. By the time I arrived, Sam had fled the scene, with cops in pursuit, and Arthur was engaged in a physical struggle with the remaining officers, in front of dozens of local residents who were powerless to intervene.

The NYPD's report stated that Arthur had a gun. This may have been true . . . or not. Regardless, it is also true that he had a permit to carry the gun and that he did not brandish it. What I remember is seeing him on the ground, motionless, unconscious, his hands cuffed behind his back, and a night-stick jammed against his throat. I remember the crowd of horrified onlookers, pleading with the cops to let him go. And I remember, most clearly of all, the intensity of the immediate aftermath, the anger and outrage of a commu-nity . . . the feeling that at any moment a riot could have erupted. And I remember feeling like I was riding a wave, pulled along inexorably by the fomenting rage.

Arthur was dead by the time he reached the hospital. An investigation absolved the officers of any wrongdoing. In the 1970s, obviously, there were no cell phones to capture the event, so eyewitness accounts were the only corroboration. But I know what I saw, what we all saw: the murder of an innocent Black man.

Chapter 6

JOHN WESLEY MILLER

I was deep into the research and writing of this memoir when I asked my father if he would mind sitting down with me and helping while I tried to fill in some of the vast blank portions of the canvas of my life. He was ninety-one years old at the time, still feisty and clear-eyed, but I wondered what he would recall, or what he would be willing to share. I questioned whether honesty and transparency could suddenly become the hallmarks of a relationship long defined by absence and anger and resentment.

"What do you want to know?" he said.

"Everything."

He shrugged, laughed in the defiant, bemused way of a man who had been mostly on his own since he was barely out of kindergarten; a man who couldn't possibly have been a good father or a good husband, because no one had ever demonstrated to him how it was done.

"Fire away," he said. "I got nothing to hide."

Snippets I had heard from others across our sprawling extended family, from great-aunts and uncles who had somehow become closer to me than my own father, who for much of my life was a shadowy presence: as disruptive and unreliable as a ghost. Stories of a family battered by scandal and broken by mental illness; of children scatted to the wind when parents and other relatives were unavailable (or unwilling) to care for them. But there was never much detail. Stories were cut short after a few sentences, usually with a roll of the eyes or a dismissive wave, as if the truth were too fantastic to grasp or too elusive to parse out with any degree of accuracy.

"Your father," my great-aunt Zeola used to say, "was dealt a bad hand." And then she'd fall silent, retreating to someplace in her mind and memory that she chose not to share. After a while, I stopped asking. And then, I stopped caring.

————————————

John Wesley Miller.

To my knowledge, the only person in our family tree seemingly important enough to have three names. Whenever he was around, or when he was addressed in absentia, it was never just John, or even John Miller. It was always "John Wesley Miller." His was the name of a statesman, or maybe a musician. An artist or a thinker, but not one willing to sit idly by as the world erupted into violence. A man who put words into action!

In truth, he was none of these things, or maybe a little of all of them, at least in his own mind. Mostly, though, he was a scared little boy, running from a childhood punctuated by abuse and neglect.

My great-grandmother, whom I knew as Mama Jin Greer, raised seventeen children, mostly in and around Charlotte,

North Carolina. One of these was my grandmother Rosana Greer. Rosana married a man named Charles Miller, who came from a family of educators. One of his cousins, whom I would meet many years down the road, while in law school in Washington, DC, achieved a degree of notoriety (including a feature story in *Jet* magazine) by graduating from Columbia University at the age of thirteen. Unfortunately, my father enjoyed none of the benefits of this association, as his family had long since been splintered by the time school became an integral part of his life.

My father was the youngest of three children born to Charles and Rosana, and by the time he came along, his mother had already become deeply indoctrinated into a congregation founded by the Reverend M. J. (Major Jealous) Divine, an African American spiritual leader who came to prominence in the South prior to the Great Depression, and who later moved to New York and founded the International Peace Mission movement, which grew from a small and predominantly Black congregation into a multiracial and international church.

Scholars and history view Father Divine with a mix of respect and skepticism. On the one hand, he was, especially in his younger days, an apparent cultist who adopted the New Thought movement and preached on the power of positive thinking in ways that, among other things, denied the inherent inequities of race—or, at the least, implied that such inequities could be overcome merely through positive thought and mind power. He was, at heart, a capitalist, as well as a charismatic preacher, embraced by congregants as "God on Earth" (a notion Father Divine certainly did not discourage). He flaunted his wealth and was no stranger to scandal—his ministry was long dogged by accusations of sexual impropriety with congregants.

On the other hand, Father Divine is also considered a civil rights activist whose network of Peace Mission centers held interracial services at a time when the vast majority of American congregations were segregated. Father Divine also used whites as secret emissaries to circumvent restrictive housing covenants and acquire homes, hotels, and beachfronts for his interracial following in northern white neighborhoods. Moreover, the Peace Mission gained notoriety for launching thriving interracial cooperative businesses. Father Divine held a "Righteous Government Convention" that called for the abolition of segregation, lynching, and capital punishment and urged an expanded government commitment to end unemployment, poverty, and hunger.

However it happened—and there is some question about this in the tattered pages of my family history—Rosana Greer found herself pulled into the orbit of Reverend Divine. She abandoned her husband and moved to New York with her three children to be part of Father Divine's growing church in Harlem.

"I was only a little kid," my father recalled. "But even then, I could tell it was more like a cult than a church. She was there all the time, day and night. We pretty much raised ourselves."

I don't know if this is true, or if time and experience have colored my father's opinion. Certainly, he has the right to feel abandoned, and if, in his eyes, the seed of that abandonment was planted in the church of Father Divine, well, who am I to argue?

Rosana was devoted entirely to the church, spent endless hours as both congregant and volunteer. Whether her relationship to Father Divine was anything other than platonic is impossible to say, as the parties involved are long since deceased. It is fair to note that across the breadth of my extended family, it has long been suggested that the Reverend M. J. Divine was the man who fathered John Wesley Miller. My father will neither deny nor confirm these rumors. I suspect he has no idea, and that my grandmother took the secret to her grave. But then, there were a great many things about Rosana Greer that my father could not possibly have known or understood.

He was seven years old when the ambulance came to the house. His mother apparently had been sick for some time, rarely leaving her bed, refusing to eat or even go to church. He watched as grim-faced adults wearing serious clothes guided her out the front door on a gurney and loaded her into the back of a waiting ambulance. One of them—a doctor, perhaps, though he couldn't be sure—said that his mother was ill and needed to be taken to a hospital. John and his siblings, Charles Miller Jr. and Willmus Miller, watched as the ambulance drove away. They had no idea what was wrong with their mother or how long she might be gone. As it turned out, the answer was "forever."

In my father's memory, some eight decades past, it all happened in a blur—a flurry of suited adults visiting the house, helping them pack clothes and driving the Miller children north through the Bronx and across the Harlem River, and into bucolic Riverdale. There, they were handed to the staff of an overflowing orphanage that was already home to some two hundred children. It was, in my father's memory, more than a little frightening. But at least they were together, Millers against the world.

Until they weren't.

It was the goal of the orphanage, and of social services, to place as many of the orphans as possible with appropriate foster families, and the Miller kids were fortunate to move rather quickly through the system. They were unfortunate in that each was assigned to a different foster family, effectively ending their sibling relationship and fracturing the family in perpetuity.

"We all ended up in Queens," my father said, "but we never saw each other."

That isn't quite true. While John Wesley lost track of his brother, he did manage to find out where his sister, Willmus, lived, and a few years later, when he was in high school, began to make semiregular visits. Not nearly enough to heal a broken family, but better than nothing.

Rosana, as it turned out, was suffering not from a physical malady but from some form of mental illness. My father was too young to ask for details of her condition; given the standard of care for such ailments at the time, none was forthcoming, and no cause for optimism was offered. She was simply whisked away to a psychiatric hospital—a "sanitarium," in the parlance of the day—where she spent the remaining years of her life. All this because of a nervous breakdown.

That's what they called it.

A nervous breakdown.

He remembers someone at the orphanage using that phrase, and he remembers thinking it didn't sound that bad. You didn't die from a nervous breakdown, right? You got better. You stopped being "nervous." Life went on. The kids would go home, and everything would be okay.

Everything was not okay. The kids never went home. To the best of his recollection, my father saw his mother only once more, during a single, brief, disquieting visit to the hospital. She was ambivalent, distant, drugged. The hospital was dark and dreary, and smelled of chemicals and cleaner. The patients were dead-eyed and dirty. There were, over time, other opportunities to visit. He declined.

How remarkable, I thought, as he related this story, that no one stepped up to take them in. There was a father . . . somewhere. There were sixteen aunts and uncles (maybe twice that many, including spouses). Three kids, suddenly adrift, and no one pulled them to shore.

"Nope," my father said. "No one."

My father's memory was good, but this seemed almost unfathomable to me, knowing what I know and what I have seen from both sides of my family—the way homes have been opened without so much as a blink of hesitation. But I have asked around, and the story has been verified, although without any definitive explanation. It simply happened.

Foster care was no Dickensian nightmare for my father. It was, he said, "okay." He had a roof over his head, food, a family that treated him well. It may not have been ideal, but it was tolerable. He graduated from high school in Queens at the age of seventeen and reconnected with his brother after a decade of estrangement. Charles and John Wesley lived together for a while in Brooklyn, while their sister went off to college, gradu-ated with honors, and got a fine job on Wall Street.

But the affliction endured by Rosana soon disrupted the lives of her children. Willmus suffered some sort of cataclys-mic event, similar to her mother's, and wound up institution-alized, with a predictably similar outcome, which is to say, a lifetime of intermittent hospitalization and confinement, fol-lowed by death. John Wesley, meanwhile, found work, adapted for a while, and then he, too, felt the crushing effects of men-tal illness, perhaps ignited or exacerbated by the trauma of his childhood. He wound up at Bellevue Hospital, where he recu-perated until, apparently out of the blue, his father reentered his life.

Charles Miller Sr. packed up his son and drove him to the Poconos, where the fresh mountain air was believed to have a healing effect on the mind and soul. It worked, too! John Wesley Miller returned to New York with his spirit rebuilt . . . ready to take on life.

"And then I got married," he said.

"Wait . . . what? You got married?"

"Yes, sir."

"To . . . Mom?"

"Hell no. That was later."

A stint in the army followed, along with a deployment to Korea, where, by my dad's own admission, the only action he saw was of the extracurricular type.

"Never got promoted. Spent too much time messing around with the Korean ladies."

Following discharge, he returned to New York—specifically, to Brooklyn—got divorced, found employment at a drugstore, and began dating the woman who would become the mother of my older half brother, John; simultaneously, he dated my mother, Flora Mae Jackson, who also had a child.

"Hey, it wasn't exclusive," my father said with a shrug. "Not like I was married or anything."

They dated for a while, broke up, got back together, and began growing a family. From roughly 1955 to 1965, Flora Mae Jackson and John Wesley Miller had three children. Add in the child each brought to the union and their family numbered five children and two adults (two more children would come later). At some point along the way they decided to get married, but that commitment, legal and moral though it might have been, did little to calm my father's wanderlust.

"I had two more kids with Donna," he said, referring to an affair long recognized but rarely discussed in our family. His frank acknowledgment, so late in life, put me back on my heels.

"Donna was Mom's best friend," I said, a reminder of the egregiousness of the offense.

"Yeah, I was crazy. And she kept coming at me. What was I supposed to do?"

My parents separated (but never divorced), and while my father remained in New York, he was little more than an occasional, disruptive figure in my life. For the first ten years or so, while we lived in Crown Heights, I barely saw him at all. Why he suddenly reappeared when we moved to the projects, I don't really know, but he brought to our family a presence that was at once authoritarian and unstable. He was an intelligent man, well-read and prone to fits of hyperarticulation and rage, who was either unemployed or underemployed his entire life. He seemed to know a lot about the world, except how to get along in it.

The combative, self-righteous personality that made him the kind of father who threatened to call the cops if I continued to sell bootleg newspapers also made him a genuinely difficult person to have in your home. Looking back on it now, I can see the telltale signs of a mood disorder. Whether this was a familial trait, or the residue of childhood trauma, or the result of a lifelong fondness for alcohol, I cannot say. Probably a bit of all three. Regardless, my father was a handful, and when he visited—whether for an hour, a day, or a week—it was like the house had been set on fire.

There were arguments that escalated into physical altercations between my parents. Sometimes others would get involved, which typically made things even worse. One of these encounters, burned into my brain, involved my father and my uncle Fred.

Uncle Fred was actually my father's uncle, and my great-uncle, but I always referred to him simply as "Uncle Fred." He was one of the seventeen children born to Mama Jin Greer, and I can only presume that some part of that tangled family history—the unwillingness to provide a home for my father and his siblings when they were orphaned—served as a catalyst for confrontation whenever they got together. Or, perhaps, my father was simply an irascible prick who brought out the worst in people.

Uncle Fred was quite old and legally blind by the time I got to know him. But he remained a proud and spirited man who was not easily intimidated. For a while, Uncle Fred came to live with us in the projects. Now, I'm not quite sure how this arrangement came to be, since Uncle Fred was part of my father's side of the family, and my father was, well . . . not really part of our family. But I didn't ask a lot of questions. We had so many relatives, fanned out across generations, on both sides of the aisle; that one of them might suddenly take up residence in our home was barely worth a shrug of recognition.

On the nights I spent with my mom and siblings at the Amsterdam Houses, I shared not just a room with Uncle Fred but also a bed. He was a storyteller, although he didn't like to talk much about my father, or the events that led to their obvious estrangement. Uncle Fred was a product of the pre–civil rights South, which might at least partially explain why he always carried a machete with him. Even while he slept, the blade was tucked beneath his pillow; sometimes I'd reach over and feel it beneath him while he snored and wonder what the hell must have happened to make Uncle Fred so paranoid.

But there is no question that my father conjured the beast in Uncle Fred.

One night, my father stopped by; as happened on many of his visits, he got into it with my mother. They argued, quietly at first, and then loudly, until their voices filled the apartment. My mother was not one to be pushed around, and her insistence on standing her ground in these disputes agitated my father into an increasingly aggressive stance, until they were standing toe to toe, yelling at each other, pointing fingers. My father, a bully and a misogynist, was not a big man, but he carried himself as though he were, always pontificating and gesticulating, and acting like he knew more than everyone else and was willing to go to war with anyone who challenged his bullshit.

Uncle Fred called my father "Little Preacher" because of his diminutive stature and his tendency to treat the home like a pulpit. But it was hardly a term of endearment, and certainly not one of respect.

"Shut the fuck up, Little Preacher!" he'd say. "You're giving me a headache."

My father, of course, would respond by turning up the volume.

On this particular night, as my father continued to berate my mother (over what, I do not recall), Uncle Fred decided that he'd heard enough. Unsheathing his machete, he waded blindly into the fray, stumbling across the kitchen, arms extended, until he crashed into the two of them and sent them flying in opposite directions.

"Not your business!" my father shouted. "Stay out of it."

Uncle Fred held the machete aloft, unable to see my father but sensing his presence.

"I'm making it my business, Little Preacher!" he said. And then he began flailing about, stabbing at the air, hacking wide, invisible swaths with his foot-long blade, as the rest of us retreated to the walls and implored him to calm down.

"Uncle Fred, it's okay," my mother said, at once appreciative of his chivalry and terrified of the potential mayhem it could provoke. "Put the knife down."

"I want him out of here!" Uncle Fred exclaimed as he lowered the machete to his side.

My father nodded, said nothing, and walked out the door. As my mother moved slowly toward Uncle Fred and put an arm around his shoulder, I could feel my heart racing in my throat.

"It's okay, Fred," she said. "He's gone."

Chapter 7

WE'RE ALL STRUGGLING

Twenty-one miles.

That's the distance between my grandmother's home in Brooklyn and Hempstead, Long Island, site of the main campus of Hofstra University.

Twenty-one miles.

I was eighteen years old, fresh out of high school, and had rarely ventured beyond the five boroughs of New York. There are a dozen different ways to navigate the tangle of freeways, bridges, and tunnels between Brooklyn and Nassau County, some with water views, some walled in by concrete and asphalt. But each invariably results in a diminution of what can plausibly be referred to as "urban."

Everything is relative, of course. If you're a freshman at Hofstra, arriving from, say, Saratoga Springs, New York, you might feel choked by the congestion and traffic and noise of western Long Island's version of suburbia. But if, like me, you are a bona fide city kid, born and raised in the projects of Manhattan and Brooklyn—if you are accustomed to the throbbing immenseness of New York—then Hofstra might as well have been Vermont. And twenty-one miles might as well have been five hundred.

"Look at all these trees," I said to my cousins Clarkson and Mary, who had volunteered to drive me to school. "It's so green."

They smiled. "Yeah, different for sure."

I wound up at Hofstra somewhat serendipitously, having rescued my high school career from the co-op program with grades sufficient to qualify for higher education but with no practical knowledge about how to navigate the application process. There were no private tutors or educational consultants in my world; there were no SAT prep programs. Or, at least, none that I knew of or could have paid to attend. I balanced work and school, took the SAT exactly once, completely cold, and then waited for someone to tell me how I could get into college. I had absolutely zero knowledge or direction about how to swim through those waters. Nor did I have any idea how I would pay for the experience if I were to gain acceptance somewhere.

Fortunately, my aunt Viola, whose education ended with high school graduation, knew a little something about the process. Her daughter's father (he never married my aunt) had another child from a different relationship. That daughter had attended Hofstra University and was familiar with the school's New Opportunities at Hofstra (NOAH) program. NOAH was (and remains) a program designed to provide opportunity for highly motivated and diverse students from underserved populations. NOAH students are economically disadvantaged and usually the first in their families to attend college. They also typically graduate from high schools that lack the resources to prepare students for competition with students from more affluent public and private schools.

There was just one catch: admission was contingent upon completing a rigorous on-campus summer program following high school graduation. I had no idea what I was getting into, no concept of what college would be like, nor the work required to be successful. I showed up on the Hofstra campus in early July, eager to prove myself but utterly clueless as to what that entailed.

What I encountered, rather suddenly, was an unsettling, demanding—and, frequently, humbling—academic boot camp. The six-week summer program was a combination of regular coursework and remedial preparation focused on basic study skills like note-taking and organization. It was presumed that most of the students in the NOAH program would be playing catch-up in the fall, and the summer session was designed to give them the best opportunity for success by closing that gap.

I bristled at the notion that I was somehow not good enough, that I had to prove myself in a way that most students did not. I was also homesick, disoriented, and I found the work, quite honestly, to be daunting. Despite the fact that all the students in the program were Black or Latino, I felt out of place. My roommate, David Thompson, was a New Yorker who had been born in Jamaica. He had a thick Caribbean accent, listened to reggae, and wore a do-rag over his dreads. He was a nice guy, and we became close friends, but in those uneasy first days of summer, he seemed, to me, like a brother from another planet.

Within hours after arriving on campus (with a single duffel bag carrying all my possessions), I found myself in a dining hall with forty-two other students, all of us disoriented and anxious. Afterward, we gathered in a lounge of the residence hall to discuss standards and expectations. I'm not sure what everyone else thought, but I expected the summer program to be a far cozier experience—more of a social indoctrination than an academic stress test. I could not have been more wrong.

"This is not a vacation," one of the counselors warned. "You are here to work, and if you don't want to work, you might as well leave right now."

The daily schedule was laid out in detail, and as I copied it into my notebook, I realized there would be no room for any of the "fun" activities I had assumed were a normal part of college life. There were classes from sunup to sundown, a break for dinner, then a couple hours for homework, and then evening sessions and discussions devoted to some book we were supposed to read or a film we would watch together. As often as not, these outside activities, for which we received no academic credit, focused on the Black experience. I figured I knew most of what I needed to know about the Black experience. I was Black, after all. I had grown up in New York. I knew racism and social inequity on a fundamental, personal level. I'd been arrested and profiled; I'd been on public assistance. What more did I need to know?

And then I started reading, and I heard the words of Frederick Douglass, Malcolm X, W. E. B. Du Bois, Pedro Albizu Campos, Marcus Garvey, and so many others—men whose voices my father had (unsuccessfully) tried to echo throughout my youth. But this time, something unlocked within me. I became hungry for more than just acceptance or transformation. I wanted *knowledge.*

But it was hard—harder than anything I had ever encountered. I found myself fatigued and mired in self-doubt. I did not fear an honest day's work, but this was different. In high school I had done just what I needed to get by in the classroom. Suddenly, people were demanding sustained intellectual effort from me, day after day, hour after hour. I had developed only a minor foundation in mathematics from my public schooling, and now I was sitting in a classroom, my head spinning as the instructor raced through advanced algebra concepts that might have seemed simple to a kid from the suburbs, but to me might as well have been astrophysics. I was assigned English papers that required legitimate research and critical thinking, rather than just the spewing of bullshit off the top of my head.

Within a few days, excitement and confidence had given way to doubt . . . and dread. Once those feelings seeped in, deep and existential, they were almost impossible to dismiss.

Why is everyone smarter than me?

Why are they having fun?

I . . . don't . . . belong . . . here!

This was all a fiction, of course, my mind playing a vicious game of impostor syndrome. In reality, just about everyone in the program experienced some version of what I was feeling—but we all had different ways of dealing with the insecurity. And yet, it was also true that some of us were better prepared than others. Most were first-generation college students who had few resources; we all had attended schools with less than stellar academic reputations. But even within that narrow subset, I came to understand that my background was among the most challenging.

And it shattered my confidence.

By the end of the first week, I wanted to go home.

"I think I'm getting out of here," I said to David one night after dinner, trying to make it sound like I was leaving a party at someone's house as opposed to making a life-altering decision.

"Nah, man, don't do that. You should stick it out," he replied in his Jamaican accent. "We're all struggling."

My mind was made up. I feigned indifference, stridency. A weird sort of confidence.

"It's okay. I don't really need this anyway. I think I'm just gonna check out."

I felt it was my duty to call Aunt Viola first, to man up and let her know I was a failure, that she had backed the wrong horse. Subconsciously, though, I believe I made that call because I knew she would have something valuable to offer on the subject. I had already called my mother and told her I was unhappy. *That's okay, baby*, she had responded. *Don't worry about it. Come on home.*

College was not the most important thing to my mother; what was important to her, in that moment, was easing her baby's pain. Aunt Viola? She was less warm and fuzzy about it.

"You want to quit?"

"Yes, ma'am."

"Already?"

"Uh-huh."

"After one week?"

Silence.

"Well . . . You could do that, I suppose," she continued. "But understand what you'll be going back to. You'll be going back to the projects—to the drugs and the crime. The shootings. You'll be going back to that job in the basement at Chase. Is that want you want?"

"I don't know. Maybe."

"Well, you'd better think about it, because you'll probably be there for the next thirty years."

There was a long pause while she let that sink in.

"No one from our family has ever graduated from college," she went on, more calmly. "You can be the first. You're not just doing this for yourself. You're doing it for your mother, your grandmother . . . for all of us."

I understood. And I stayed.

I completed the program. I made some good friends. And I found a mentor, probably the first person outside of my family who believed in me and supported me, but also held me to a standard I wasn't even sure I could meet. Frank Smith was the director of the NOAH program (we all called him Dean Smith), as well as an alumnus. An African American man who stood more than six feet tall and weighed close to 250 pounds, Frank was both physically and intellectually impressive. He had the rare ability to be both compassionate and demanding. Frank helped me develop the academic and social skills necessary for success not just in college but in the marketplace. He encouraged me to be active in my community and to serve the country at large. It's fair to say that I would not be where I am without Frank Smith's encouragement and support.

It would also be fair to say that ours was a sometimes contentious relationship, for Frank believed in and administered tough love in a manner that I had never received from an adult male. I never told him that I came within a breath of quitting in that first week, but I knew there were others who thought about quitting as well, both during the summer program and at other times in their college careers. Frank rarely tried to talk anyone out of leaving; it simply wasn't his nature, nor his role. Instead, he talked often and passionately about the struggles and challenges of Black people in America, and how fortunate we were to have the opportunity that had been presented to us.

"There are a lot of kids out there who would love to trade places with you," he'd say. "They can't afford to go to college. They're stuck. Think about that. Think about the responsibility."

This was not delivered with the exuberance of a cheerleader but rather with the solemnity of a leader. Dean Smith was not even thirty years old at the time, but he seemed to have wisdom and experience far beyond his years. If you wanted to quit, he would not talk you out of it; he would let you make the decision. But he was not shy about hitting you in the face with the reality of the situation: that you weren't just quitting on yourself; you were quitting on your family, your friends, and Black people everywhere who weren't fortunate enough to have been handed a key to a better life. Basically, it was the same message I received from Aunt Viola, and their voices, in tandem, had a profound impact on my attitude and resilience.

I could not afford to be weak. I could not quit.

Six weeks is not a long time, but in that environment, at once collegial and intensely competitive, relationships were formed that lasted a lifetime. David, whose appearance and demeanor unmoored me the day we met, became my best friend throughout college. Years later, after I graduated from law school, some of the counselors in the NOAH summer program became business partners of mine. I don't know how to explain this except to say that the bonds forged in such an intensely challenging arena are not easily broken. Dean Smith built a cohesive and supportive environment, one in which the students competed with each other for grades but also lifted each other and pulled each other along. It wasn't enough to do well; your peers had to succeed, for their failure was yours—a collective breakdown in the system, and one for which we all bore some responsibility. I had never experienced such a feeling of inclusion. Truthfully, I never experienced it again. The NOAH summer program was brutal and unique, and it laid the foundation for everything I was able to accomplish thereafter.

In ways larger than I even realized at the time, it changed me.

That September, I formally enrolled as a freshman at Hofstra. It was then that the culture shock began in earnest. I lived in a triple that year with two suburban kids—one from Virginia, the other, a wrestler, from California—who had graduated from good schools and acted like they had never met a Black person. And I'd definitely never been around so many white folks. We might as well have been from different worlds. Socially, I felt out of place and frequently sought the familiarity of friendships with other African American students from the NOAH program.

There were roughly eleven thousand students at Hofstra, and the vast majority were white and middle class. There was a very small African American population, and a significant percentage of those students were enrolled through the NOAH program. We stuck together almost by default, our friendships having been forged during the summer program and solidified when we got on campus and realized what an overwhelmingly white universe we had entered (this was less apparent in the summer, when we had been cloistered). But we were a family. Despite the general underrepresentation of students of color, I could almost count on there being one or two other Black or Latino students in the class. We always knew each other, sat next to each other, shared notes and ideas (and the occasional wry observation). The very fact of our *otherness* brought us closer together and made us stronger.

Whatever meager social life I had during my freshman year in college revolved almost entirely around the friendships I had formed through the NOAH program. Mostly, though, I studied. Hard.

Other students seemed to have endless appetites for partying—these kids consumed more drugs than a lot of the people I knew back in the projects. Some of them were dealing, too. I stayed away from all of that. I remember sitting at my desk studying one evening when my roommates went out (which they did most nights). They returned four or five hours later, stoned, drunk. I was still in the same spot.

"Jesus, man, you still working?" one of them said.

"Uh-huh."

"You need to ease up and have some fun." They both laughed.

The Hofstra campus was undeniably beautiful. So many perfectly maintained buildings spread out across green space. Though I lived in a triple, at least I had my own bed. While others complained about cafeteria food, I thought it was fine. And I could eat as much as I wanted, a privilege I had rarely known while growing up.

Another memory, also first semester: I left the library at midnight, at the very moment it closed. When I walked out the door, I was alone in the darkness, and it occurred to me then that I had been the very last student to leave the building. I started to walk back to my dorm. The campus was stone silent. I looked around at the half-lit buildings and drank in the quiet.

They do not think you belong here. They don't think you're good enough.

I remembered a quote from Frederick Douglass: "If there is no struggle, there is no progress."

I walked back to my dorm room, which reeked of weed and sweat. My roommates were sound asleep, still in their clothes.

Over time, I came to understand that while life rarely offers an even playing field, there are things you can do to improve your odds of success, and to change the outcome. I couldn't help that I came from the projects, or that I didn't go to an expensive private school. I couldn't help that I grew up mostly without a father, or that many of my friends had gotten into drugs or gone to jail. Or that some had been killed. There was nothing I could do about the fact that the two guys sleeping in my room had been granted a massive head start in life. But there was something else I could do.

I could outwork them.

Most people, I realized shortly after I got to Hofstra, do the bare minimum in life to get by. They expect positive results without putting in much effort because life, generally speaking, has been easy for them. I expected nothing, because nothing had ever been handed to me.

"I'm going to catch you," I whispered. "Just watch me."

Another poem, "The Ladder of St. Augustine," by Henry Wadsworth Longfellow, to which I had been introduced during my NOAH summer at Hofstra, rang in my mind as I pushed ahead:

> *The heights by great men reached and kept*
> *Were not attained by sudden flight,*
> *But they, while their companions slept,*
> *Were toiling upward in the night.*

I don't mean to give the impression that my roommates were racists, or even antagonistic. To be precise, there simply wasn't any connection at all. We were totally different, and none of us had any great desire to bridge those differences. I was no more interested in trying to understand their whiteness (and their privilege, which I resented) than they were interested in trying to understand my Blackness, and my lack of privilege. I suppose their efforts came in the way of partying, of encouraging me to embrace the more decadent aspects of becoming a college student and getting away from home. How could they possibly have known what I had encountered in the projects? The crime and violence and death. To me, drug use was still not something you did casually on a Friday night after a week of classes. It was a lifestyle choice, and a terrible one at that, inextricably linked to poverty and prison. It was a black hole from which you'd never escape.

Point of view is everything, and ours could not have been more dissimilar.

I sought refuge in the predictability and formality of the classroom, becoming the antithesis of the lazy, indifferent student I had been in high school. Almost immediately, the hard work paid off, as I began to accumulate the sort of consistently strong grades that boosted my confidence, as well as my GPA. Still, there was pushback in the form of racism that might have been more subtle than what I encountered as a kid but was no less degrading. Early in the first semester, after I received a few high marks on some tests in an introductory accounting class, the professor summoned me to his office.

"Have you taken Accounting One before?" he asked. This was a ridiculous question, as I was a freshman—I can only presume he had not even taken the time to read my basic student bio.

"No, sir. Why?"

"Oh, it's just that you seem to have a really strong grasp of the material."

Uh-huh.

"Thank you," I said. "I work hard."

"Okay, well . . . keep it up," he said, while giving me a look that spoke volumes. What he meant, of course, was this: *I can't believe a Black kid is this good at accounting.*

To be fair—or, at least, objective—accounting classes at Hofstra (and at most universities) were not particularly popular with Black students, so perhaps he was unaccustomed to seeing a nonwhite face in his classroom, a fact that surely challenged his ability to view my efforts through a lens unclouded by racism. Regardless, I let it roll off my back.

By the time my freshman year came to an end, I was a dean's list student with a small but close-knit social circle. I no longer felt like a fish out of water. It hadn't been easy, but by this point I understood what was required to be successful in college. For me, a smart but far-from-brilliant kid who was mostly unprepared for the academic rigors of higher education, the formula was simple: Work your ass off. Every day. It was a matter of diligence and execution, and knowing that those things were within my power to control helped ease my anxiety considerably.

I wasn't going to quit, and I wasn't going to fail.

There was, however, the issue of money to consider. While in school, I could rely on the meal plan for sustenance, and I had a small amount of personal savings to draw upon. My family would also send food stamps so I could buy some extra groceries to keep in my dorm room. But almost all of that was gone now. I needed a summer job not just to support myself during the time I'd be home, but also to help defray expenses in my sophomore year. The NOAH scholarship was generous, covering tuition, room and board, and books, but I still needed to *live*. One of the hardest things about being a poor kid at a private university is that you often feel isolated or ostracized not just because of your financial aid package or scholarship but because you can't even scrape together ten bucks to go out for pizza on a Friday night. Meanwhile, your roommates seem to have a bottomless allowance—credit cards, cars, nice clothes. It's like you're walking around with the word *POOR* stamped on your back.

But I had a plan.

Late in my freshman year, a representative from the Gold Coast Book Company visited campus, hoping to recruit eager college kids to sell his company's product: encyclopedias. What I did not realize at the time was that selling encyclopedias, door-to-door, to an indifferent or hostile clientele, was one of the most challenging, depressing, impractical ways to earn a living that anyone has ever devised. I just sat there with my friend Sabir, listening to the Gold Coast Book Company guy, in his shiny suit, with his sparkling watch and equally sparkling teeth, and his slicked-back hair, talking about how much money we could make and what a valuable product we'd be representing, and I could hear cash registers ringing.

Easy money.

There it was again. As much of a lie as it ever was.

"What do you think?" I said to Sabir as the presentation came to an end.

He smiled. "I think we're going to be rich."

The recruiting pitch centered around the premise that wealthy folks in suburban neighborhoods all wanted their kids to be well educated, and to have every possible advantage while going through school and applying to college. In the dark days before the information superhighway was constructed, research was conducted in the dusty stacks of libraries or while hunkered over reams of microfiche. You didn't just fire up the laptop and Bing or Google your subject of choice.

There was no Wikipedia.

There were, instead, encyclopedias. Thick volumes of information, as big as cinder blocks, thousands of pages of often arcane information, arranged chronologically, alphabetically, or simply by topic. People wanted encyclopedias in their homes. They *needed* encyclopedias! And they were willing to pay hundreds, if not thousands of dollars for the privilege and security of knowledge.

Or so we were led to believe.

This may in fact have been true in the pristine mansions of the upper-crust New York City suburbs: places like Scarsdale and Rye, Sag Harbor and Greenwich. I can't say for sure because the Gold Coast Book Company did not send Sabir and me to those places, or to any other suburbs even remotely similar.

"Orlando," I told my mother. "That's where we're going."

"Orlando?" she repeated. "Orlando . . . Florida?"

"Uh-huh," I said proudly, as if I was about to embark on an epic adventure that would be the envy of my family and friends.

"Well, that figures. Send the Black kids to sell to other Black people."

"I don't think it's like that, Mommy. They said it's a good market. We'll sell a ton of books."

"I'm sure you will, dear."

They told us we'd be "self-employed," a designation that, as a former newspaper bootlegger, appealed to my sense of entrepreneurship. They'd give us some samples to take into the living rooms of friendly, welcoming families; we'd sell a bunch of books and keep a percentage of the gross. Of course, being self-employed, we were not privy to such luxuries as an office, or a living space, or even travel to our assigned territory.

Sabir and I scraped up enough money for two tickets from the Port Authority Bus Terminal to Orlando, a distance of some eleven hundred miles, with about seventy-five stops along the way. We found shelter at a youth hostel that charged twenty-five bucks a week for one of six cots in a shared bedroom. It was a dark, filthy place, with mold on the walls and rat droppings in the kitchen. Having grown up in the projects, I was not unfamiliar with cockroaches, but the winged beasts in Orlando made New York roaches look like mosquitoes. You could actually hear them scurrying about: *clackety-clackety-clackety-clack.*

The term *youth hostel*, I discovered, was largely euphemistic, conjuring images of fresh-faced college kids backpacking across Europe. In reality, our place in Orlando was indistinguishable from a homeless shelter, with a mix of drug addicts, runaways, and prostitutes sharing living quarters with the occasional misguided college kid—like us.

But we were undaunted. We put on crisp pants and pressed shirts—sweated through both before we reached the end of the driveway—and went out the first day to our assigned territory, a poor suburban neighborhood of single-story tract homes and trailers. The residents were uniformly Black. Surprisingly, almost no one slammed their doors in our faces. For the most part, they welcomed us into their homes and listened patiently as we read from a prepared script that offered the promise of knowledge and trans-formation.

A better life for you and your family.

All for just five easy payments of $99 a month.

"Honey, you seem like nice boys," the first woman said. "But do I look like I got five hundred dollars for encyclo-pedias?"

It felt like a trick question. To say yes would be to wave the flag of ignorance. To say no would be an insult. So I just stood there silently, staring at the floor.

"Good luck, boys," she said. "Try to stay cool out there."

That was as good as it got. We must have visited a dozen homes that first day, and the closest we came to a sale was when one woman offered to revisit the issue on the fifteenth, when her welfare check came in.

We never went back. After a few days Sabir got discour-aged to the point that he wouldn't leave the youth hostel.

"This isn't working out," he said.

"Give it some time, man. It'll get better."

He shook his head. "I'm sorry. I'm going home."

By the end of the week, Sabir's parents had sent him enough money for a plane ticket, and he was gone. I had no such options. There was no one to call, no one to ask for money. I wasn't quite ready to acknowledge defeat, anyway, so I stayed for another two weeks, rising early, putting on my increasingly wrinkled and sweat-stained sales outfit, and trudging through the poor neighborhoods of a swamp-like suburban Orlando. I made a few sales—not for the full amount but for much smaller, partial orders that put enough money in my pocket to pay rent and get some food—tuna fish and crackers, mostly. I met one family that took pity on me—not only bought a few books but invited me to dinner and then on a day trip to Disney World.

Eventually, I bought a bus ticket home, along with a six-pack of Coca-Cola and some cookies, and returned to New York. I didn't even bother calling my family in advance because I was both embarrassed and proud: I did not want to make them feel as though they had to send me money. I'd gotten myself into this mess, and I would get myself out.

Twenty-four hours later I was back in New York. I got a job at McDonald's, minimum wage, flipping burgers and serving fries. It seemed easy by comparison, and I was grateful for the paycheck—small but reliable—that was waiting for me at the end of every week.

Chapter 8

BROTHERHOOD

By September, I was eager for the start of school. Secure in the knowledge that I could handle the rigors of academia and buoyed by several strong friendships, I returned to Hofstra mostly unburdened by the anxiety and insecurity that had nearly derailed my college career before it had even begun. If anything, I suffered from a degree of confidence—if not hubris—that at times proved equally troublesome.

Like a lot of college kids, I decided to join a fraternity. I never considered pledging to a white fraternity and instead narrowed my choices to the handful of national African American fraternities that had chapters on campus, Alpha Phi Alpha (which counted Martin Luther King Jr. among its members) being one of the most well-known, along with a newer, local fraternity called Malik Sigma Psi, which had been founded on May 13, 1977, at the C. W. Post campus of Long Island University.

Malik Sigma Psi was controversial on campus, as it presented a strong African American sensibility. Rather than refer to themselves as Black Greeks, its members preferred the term African fraternalists. The name itself—Malik Sigma Psi—combined elements of the Muslim name of Malcolm X (el-Hajj Malik el-Shabazz) with the more traditional Greek letters Sigma and Psi. The fraternity first considered an entirely Swahili name but modified its moniker to meet guidelines for Greek life established by most colleges and universities, a concession that perhaps mitigated some of the backlash from those who would presume the fraternity was a radical organization. The truth, however, is that Malik Sigma Psi *was* a somewhat radical organization, guided by the spirit of African fraternalism. As such, it became a political and emotional lightning rod on the overwhelmingly white Hofstra campus. The fraternity's name was changed to simply MALIK in 2002, and in its modern public literature, one can easily see the sort of bold pronouncements that, while virtually unimpeachable today, would have sparked fear and trepidation among traditionally white institutions (such as universities and fraternities), particularly in the turbulent '70s, when memory of the civil rights movement was still fresh . . . and raw.

> The MALIK Fraternity, Inc. subscribes to a set of beliefs and principles that have been codified and defined as "African Fraternalism." The title MALIK, being a Swahili word meaning "King or Ruler," embodies this spirit. African Fraternalism includes such beliefs as the African origin of civilization, reclaiming the stolen legacy of African knowledge, the oneness of all African peoples, the importance of

ritual and initiation, the value of a male ritual kinship system, respect for and seeking equal partnership with women, the reception and cultivation of the Spirit of Learning, the necessity of serving the community, the calling to work on one's personal and spiritual development, and the study and promotion of "Malikology," and the usage of "African Symbology."

Simply put, white America was terrified of Black America, and Malik Sigma Psi saw no reason to apologize for exacerbating that discomfort. It was, in fact, necessary. It was progress.

After giving the matter considerable thought, I chose to join Malik Sigma Psi. As with all fraternities, pledges underwent various initiation rites, most of which will remain undocumented here. One of the tamer traditions was that all pledges walk in a line together, as a unit, when traversing the campus. This was less about humiliation and subjugation than it was a show of solidarity, a message to the senior members of the fraternity, and to the campus at large, that we were brothers, never to be divided or separated. A phalanx of pledges—particularly if all the men were Black—could be an intimidating sight.

Or a target.

We were walking in this fashion one Saturday night when we were approached by a group of big white guys, football players, mostly. They were loud, drunk, antagonistic in that stupid way of college kids who've partied a little too hard. They knew who we were, and they knew the boundaries and expectations: pledges walking together were compelled to defend their line against interlopers. Usually, there was nothing to defend, but on this night, one of the football players decided to test the system. He got down in a three-point stance, then let out a yell and charged at the line, breaking through it and sending several pledges flying.

My response was instantaneous. As the guy struggled to his feet, I attacked him, unleashing a hailstorm of punches to his face before he even knew what hit him. Now, I was not a big man, maybe five foot eight, 160 pounds. This guy had me by several inches and at least fifty pounds, but he was drunk and slow. By the time he realized what was happening, the fight was broken up and we were pulled apart. But by then, his nose was bloodied and his face knotted up.

I had no regret over standing up for myself and my brothers against the onslaught of a drunken bully. In that situation, at that moment, I did not consider turning the other cheek to be an option. Sometimes you have to defend yourself. But there are consequences to actions, and now I had put myself in a position where someone else controlled my destiny.

Surprisingly, reason prevailed. My status as one of the top students on campus worked in my favor, as did the fact that numerous witnesses offered the rather obvious assessment that I was not the instigator but merely one who acted in self-defense. This wasn't quite true. I don't think the football player intended to cause any further harm, and my reaction was born of nothing so much as rage. But it was, in the end, determined to be a reasonable amount of rage.

We both got off with a warning and moved on.

Malik Sigma Psi was a fraternity without walls, so to speak, its membership rooted more in philosophy and community than residential life. It was among the fraternities most actively engaged in social initiatives, and the least likely to engage in *Animal House*–style reverie (Saturday night keg parties, for example, were never near the top of our priorities, nor even near the bottom). We used to go to high schools and elementary schools in underserved communities and speak to kids about opportunity and responsibility. Eventually, I became president of the organization, and it was vitally important to me that these kids were aware of the world beyond their neighborhoods; that, unlike so many of my childhood friends, they didn't feel trapped by race and economics and other circumstances beyond their control.

At one point, we sponsored a big show on campus, the profits from which financed a program that allowed us to bus in high school students for a "college experience." And it wasn't just for male students; an equal number of female students participated in the program, spending the weekend with our sister organization. For many of these kids, the idea of college was illusory (just as it had been for me), but we tried to make it real . . . attainable. Simply by giving them a taste of college life—by showing them that students of color, many from poor backgrounds, were not just represented at Hofstra but achieving at a high level—we gave them hope.

We gave them a reason to believe that their dreams, when paired with hard work, resiliency, and mentorship, could indeed become reality.

I was not just surviving college—I was thriving. I had worked hard to build myself into a leader among men, but then I got a preview of life thereafter. A dose of the real world.

While taking Accounting II, in my sophomore year, I experienced an incident similar to that which I experienced as a freshman, in my first accounting class—got a few strong grades, established myself as one of the best students in the class, got summoned to the professor's office and asked whether this was my second go-around, because, you know, the only way a Black kid could know the material this well is if he had taken the class before, didn't do so well, but probably absorbed enough to do better on the next pass.

"No, sir, I just like accounting."

He ran a hand through his hair. "Really?"

"Yes, sir. I'm planning to major in accounting."

"That's . . . unusual," he said, leaving the obvious unstated.

"Sir?"

"Oh, I mean. It's just that . . . never mind."

He paused, changed directions.

"Have you thought about applying for a scholarship?"

"I'm already on scholarship," I said.

"Really?"

"I'm in the NOAH program."

A subtle lift of the eyebrow. A sigh. "I see."

"But if there's anything else I could do to earn some money, that would be great."

He pursed his lips, thought for a moment. "We could always use another tutor . . . if you think you're up to it."

I got into the honor society, which solidified my status as a serious student, and in the spring I began working in the office for academic support as a peer tutor. It was there that my predilection for hustling, honed through years in the projects, bubbled to the surface and got me in trouble. See, the thing about being a tutor was that you only got paid if you actually did the tutoring. You could set aside a block of time and a student could make an appointment to work with you, but if the student didn't show up, you didn't get paid.

This happened. A lot.

After a while, it really started to get on my nerves. I would arrange my own studying schedule around tutoring assignments, and it seemed unfair that I would make this commitment but not get paid just because the student failed to meet his or her responsibility. But rules were rules. In order to get paid, I had to sign a timesheet, as did the person I was supposed to be tutoring. After a few cancellations and missed appointments, I started chasing down the no-shows.

"Look, it's not my business if you don't want my help," I said. "But if you make an appointment for a session, you need to show up. If you don't want to stay, that's up to you. But I need you to sign the timesheet."

This was flawed logic on my part, not a big leap from the logic that told me it was acceptable to steal a stack of as-yet-unclaimed newspapers on a city street and sell them as if they were my own. For pure profit. Granted, one example is theft; the other is, well . . . somewhat fraudulent, maybe. Regardless, it was wrong, but I needed the money, and I was angry, and old habits—old ways of thinking—sometimes die hard.

It only happened three or four times, but that was enough to raise a red flag. Predictably, I got caught, and very quickly the wheels of justice were set in motion. I found myself sitting in Dean Smith's office, a stack of timesheets fanned out on his desk. We sat across from each other in silence for what felt like several minutes as he stared at the timesheets, then stared at me . . . and then stared again at the timesheets. Finally, he let out a sigh of exasperation.

"You turned these in, correct?"

"Yes, I did."

"You signed the timesheets, the student signed the timesheets, but no service was provided?"

"That's right." I didn't try to manipulate the scenario or even offer any sort of explanation, beyond that which I believed to be true.

"This is stealing, Bruce. It's plain old theft. And you know it."

I did not know it. To my eyes, there was nuance to this situation that Frank Smith seemed to be missing.

"With all due respect, Dean Smith, I disagree. I was in the office, on time, waiting for these students to show up. I shouldn't have money taken out of my pocket because of their laziness."

He shook his head in what I can only describe as a paternal sort of way; a motion infused less with anger than disappointment.

"That's a *rationalization*, not a defense. If you had a problem, you should have gone to one of the counselors in the academic support office and explained it to them. Or you should have come to me. But this"—he waved at the timesheets—"this is wrong."

The meeting ended as badly as it had begun, with Frank shaken not only by what I had done but my seeming inability to grasp the moral implications. He told me, in no uncertain terms, that he was inclined to throw me out of school.

Over the next few weeks, however, while giving the matter time to percolate, Dean Smith faced opposition from other students and faculty members. The argument against expulsion hinged on the fact that I was one of the highest-performing students in the accounting program. To date, my academic record was impeccable. And while I clearly had made a serious mistake, it wasn't like I was running a scam. On each occasion, I had shown up to fulfill my obligation as a tutor. I wanted to be paid for meeting my end of the bargain.

Eventually the matter was kicked all the way up to the office of the provost, who kicked it right back down to the dean of the NOAH program.

In the end, thanks to the support of so many students and teachers, and the fact that Frank still believed in me, I was given a reprieve. The lesson, once again: never leave your future in the hands of someone else. I had made a poor decision, the ramifications of which could have undercut everything I had worked so hard to achieve. It was a harsh lesson in accountability, but one that could have turned out much worse.

In the summer after my sophomore year, I got a job working for my old employer Chase Bank, although not in the basement making copies, but rather as a customer service associate (known in the parlance of the day as a "bank teller") at a branch on West Twenty-Third Street. It wasn't the greatest summer job, but it sure beat selling encyclopedias in the sweltering Florida suburbs. The pay was pretty good, the air-conditioning worked flawlessly, and after a few days of training, I could practically do the job in my sleep. Moreover, as an accounting major, a bank position would be a nice line to have on my résumé after graduation.

Because the job was in Manhattan, I moved back into my old room at my mother's place in the Amsterdam Houses. But I kept firm roots in Brooklyn with Aunt Viola and, even more so, my grandmother Mamie. I visited her often in Brooklyn, and we talked on the phone every day—and I mean . . . *every day.* On Wednesday, August 10, 1983—my twenty-first birthday—I called her before going to work. She wished me a happy birthday, told me how much she loved me, and how proud of me she was. She did this all the time, but the words never got old.

"You'll be coming over tonight, right?" she asked.

"I don't think so, Grandmama. Long day at work. I'll probably just see you over the weekend."

"I was going to make cookies."

I smiled. "That's okay, Grandmama. You don't have to do that."

"It's no trouble. Not for you."

"Why don't you just wait, and we'll celebrate on Saturday."

"Okay," she said. "Have a wonderful day."

"I will. I love you."

"Love you, too."

Had I known those were the last words I'd ever hear her say, I might have stretched out the conversation. I would have told her how much she meant to me, how safe I always felt in her presence, and what a sturdy, calming influence she had been; how she had basically saved my life by taking me in when I was high school. But we never have advance notice on these things, do we? They just happen.

After work I went out with some friends and celebrated my birthday at a bar near Broadway and Sixty-Eighth. When

I got home that night, my mother was crying. She was surrounded by a mix of relatives and friends, all of them hugging her, consoling her.

"Mommy," I said. "What's going on?

"It's your grandmother," she said. "She's had a heart attack . . . or something."

"Is she okay?"

There was no answer, just more crying, as my mother burrowed her head into my chest.

In those days you couldn't just track down people or information with a few simple clicks of a smartphone. Aunt Viola had called with the message, but now the land line at her apartment rang endlessly, as did the phone at my grandmother's home. The only way to find out what had happened was to get to Brooklyn, so we all piled into a van owned by my sister's boyfriend and raced down the West Side Highway.

When we arrived, Grandmama was still in her bed, and one of my uncles was standing over her, slapping her in the face, gently at first, and then harder, shouting, "Wake up, Mama! Wake up!" Tears streamed down his face as he pulled the covers up and walked away. I stood a good distance away, wanting to know what was happening but afraid to look.

An ambulance had been summoned some time ago, my uncle reported, but had yet to arrive. This was not uncommon in poorer neighborhoods, where concern over payment, lack of adequate health insurance, and a paucity of qualified EMTs often led to interminable waits for assistance, even in the most critical situations.

Eventually, they showed up, spent a few short minutes in her bedroom, and then told us she had passed. They could not take the body, as they were responsible only for the living, or the barely living. My grandmother no longer fit that description. Someone from the coroner's office would be there soon, they said, to take her to the morgue. They apologized perfunctorily for the inconvenience and left, and as they walked out the door, I thought, *My God, how do you do this every day?*

One by one, as we waited for the morgue truck to arrive, family members walked into the bedroom to say goodbye. My mother, Aunt Viola, my cousins Phillip and LaTasha. They wept and held Grandmama's hand; they brushed back her hair. They kissed her on the cheek. They told her how much they loved her and how much she meant to the family. I saw this from a distance, through a shimmering haze of tears, in furtive, denying glances. I would not go into the room. I did not want to see her like this. Instead, I stood in the kitchen, thinking of all the times I had sat at that table and eaten meals prepared by Grandmama. I wandered over to the window and looked out at the street below and thought of how many times I had seen her standing in this very same spot, at the window, smiling, as I ran up the street after school, the smell of freshly baked cookies wafting into the open air.

That's the way I wanted to remember her: full of life and love.

I waited until the men finished their grisly work, lifting her off the bed and zipping her into a black bag. I could hear it all happening, but I did not watch. I was twenty-one years old. A grown man. Officially, legally, an adult.

I was also, in that moment, a coward. In the presence of Grandmama's fleeing spirit, I was a lost and scared little boy.

A few days later, at her memorial service, I spent most of the afternoon and evening outside, standing on the front steps, shaking hands with well-wishers, an endless parade of relatives and friends and acquaintances, many of whom I did not even know. This, I thought, was a purposeful life; this was a woman who made a difference. But I could not go inside, not until they closed the casket. Once this was done, however, I walked into the funeral home and took my place at the front of the room, next to the flowers and the cards and the casket.

"I'd like to speak," I said. There were nods all around, a few smiles, lots of tears. I proceeded to deliver the first eulogy of my young life. My voice broke a few times, but I got through it. Near the end, I talked about something we had discussed a lot over the years: my desire, at first juvenile and based on Hollywood fantasy, but now more tangible, given that I was halfway through a promising academic career.

"I always said I wanted to be a lawyer, right, Grandmama? Like Perry Mason?" Everyone laughed. "Well, I'm going to do it. And I'm going to do it for you. I love you, Grandmama."

While I continued to excel academically at Hofstra, overall growth came in fits and starts, in part because of the massive chip I carried on my shoulder. I had something to prove—to my professors, my fellow students, the folks back home in Brooklyn and Manhattan. Some of this was related to race—to a burning desire to prove that I could overcome the preconceptions and bigotry of the white institutions that held my fate in their hands. But not all of it. Some of it was tied into a complex stew of emotions stemming from where I had grown up, and the people I had left behind, although I hadn't completely left them, or their world. I went home often, and on those visits, I wanted to prove that I had transcended my upbringing but remained connected to it, as well. This had the odd effect of provoking a sort of dissonance both at school and at home.

I belonged nowhere.

And everywhere.

Even in the wake of a brawl and an integrity issue—either of which could have gotten me tossed out of school—I remained combative, unwilling to shrink from confrontations large or small, in the classroom or on the street.

I began taking karate classes in my spare time at Hofstra, got pretty good at it, or so I thought. One time, I went home and ran into a guy who was widely known as the bully of the housing project. His name was Tyronne, and he'd been a thorn in my side for years, always making fun of me, threatening me, extorting money from me. He was less of an agitation after I moved to Brooklyn, and especially when I went off to college, but he didn't exactly disappear; he just found other targets.

On this particular day, I saw Tyronne from a distance on Amsterdam Avenue, walking straight toward me. By Sixty-Second Street, we were within shouting distance of each other. He glared at me, probably expected me to turn and run. I kept walking until we were separated by only a few feet. He held his hands out to the side, as if to say, *What are you gonna do?* I knew by then that if you were serious about fighting, you didn't say anything. The best strategy was to throw the first punch and make it a good one. Which is exactly what I did. But Tyronne was much bigger than me, roughly six foot three, 210 pounds, and while bullies are known for quitting when someone finally stands up to them, Tyronne was not inclined to surrender.

We fought for two city blocks, all the way to Sixty-Fourth Street, wrestling and punching and choking each other all the way. We'd fall, get up, throw some more punches, fall again, and then catch our breath and continue the violent dance. A crowd gathered and began cheering me on. It was like we were in middle school, and I was the quiet kid on the playground who decided he'd had enough and fought back against the bully who'd been terrorizing the entire school. Everyone wanted to see Tyronne go down.

The fight ended with Tyronne exhausted, unable to defend himself and saying he'd had enough. I remember people applauding as I walked toward my mother's place, dirty, sweaty, and bruised, but triumphant nevertheless. It didn't occur to me then what I had risked—the possibility that Tyronne might have beaten me up, or worse, had a gun; or that I might have hurt him so badly that charges would be filed; or that the cops would get word of the ruckus and show up and put both of us in jail for assault. There were a dozen ways it could have gone wrong and altered the trajectory of my life. I just got lucky.

Not long after that I went to a supermarket in a rough neighborhood near Hofstra. While shopping, some guy accidentally bumped into me. Rather than let it go, I immediately confronted him.

"Hey, man, what's that about?"

The guy offered a half-assed apology, tried to go on with his shopping. I pressed the issue, asked him if he wanted to step outside and settle things like men. I had kicked Tyronne's ass. I had beaten up a drunk football player at school. Hell, I knew karate! I wasn't worried.

We went outside. I threw the first punch, as usual. It didn't land. He threw the next punch. It did land. Two minutes into the fight, I was exhausted and getting pummeled and thinking to myself, *God, please let somebody stop this!* It went on for a bit longer, until I was basically balled up, trying to shield my face, so fatigued I could barely breathe. Finally, someone dragged him off.

That was the last fistfight I was ever involved in. Sometimes you learn the hard way.

Overall, college was a mixed experience, but it was an *important* experience. At Hofstra, I learned how to be a student, and to put in the time and the work to chart my own path. I learned that there are no shortcuts in life, that anything worthwhile requires consistent effort—and *persistent* effort. I grew up. I took responsibility. I learned to seek out the advice and wisdom of people smarter than I was. I learned the importance of reciprocity and compromise; even more important, I learned how to *pay it forward*, to embrace the notion that I wasn't an island, that I was part of something bigger, and that whatever success I might enjoy in life carried with it an implicit contract to help others.

I also kept that promise to my grandmother. In the spring of 1985 I received my diploma, with honors. I was one of the top students in my class, but more important, I was the first college graduate in my family. It was a powerful moment, more emotional than I had anticipated, in part because, while more than a dozen members of my extended family were in attendance, the person who would have appreciated it the most was not there to see it, and her absence was palpable.

I thought about what Aunt Viola used to say about the extraordinary life my grandmother had led and the struggles she had endured.

"It was tough down there in the South," she'd say. "The racism was awful. You couldn't look white people in the eye. You had to address them as 'sir' or 'ma'am'. Your grandmother had to clean people's houses and didn't have time to clean her own house. It was hard." Then she'd pause. "And her grandmother, your great-great-grandmother, was a slave."

I thought about Grandmama as I clutched my diploma and took pictures with the rest of the family. There were a lot of tears, not just because they were proud of me but because so many of them had played a role—helping me buy clothes, sharing their food stamps, offering emotional support. I felt proud to be setting an example, letting others in my family know that college was not just possible but realistic. If I could do it, so could they. I tried to picture my grandmother there with us, smiling. And I thought about what I would say.

Look, Grandmama! Someone born through you did this. Without you, I'm not here. Without you, I never get this opportunity. It doesn't happen. This is for you.

Chapter 9

GEORGETOWN

After graduation, I had solid job offers from some of the best accounting firms in the country but instead decided to enroll in law school. Deathbed promises to Grandmama notwithstanding, this was not a decision made without angst. For me, with what I'd come from, turning down a job with a Big Eight accounting firm felt like turning down an NBA contract. One of the recruiters, a Black woman in her forties from Arthur Andersen, laid out all the inducements: a great starting salary, the potential to advance rapidly, a promise of wealth and security. For just about every accounting major at Hofstra, or any other college for that matter, this was an ideal scenario—but while I was flattered to receive the offer and tempted by the promise of money (not *easy money*, it should be noted), I felt a sense of ambivalence.

It felt like . . . settling.

"What's wrong?" the recruiter had asked, smiling politely.

"I'm sorry?"

"Well, you just don't seem very enthusiastic about our offer. Most students in your position would be thrilled."

"I know, and I appreciate your interest very much. It's just that I'm not sure it's right for me."

"Can I ask you a question?" she said.

"Of course."

"What do you want to do with your life?"

It seemed like the simplest question, and one I had been taught to anticipate during interviews, but coming from her in this setting, it gave me pause. She was after something deeper than the usual response, which I coughed up anyway.

"I want to be successful. I want to help take care of my family."

She nodded. "Yes, I'm sure you do. That's not what I'm talking about."

"Ma'am?"

"What do you *want?* What will make you happy? What excites you?" She stopped, drummed her fingers on the desk. "God willing, you'll be working for the next forty years, Bruce. At least. Believe me, if you don't love your job—if it's just a paycheck—that forty years will drag."

Except she didn't just say drag. Instead, she stretched out the word for what felt like three syllables.

"Draaaaaaag."

I thought about the old guys I met at Chase, doing the same job, day after day, week after week, year after year. And hating it. Counting the days till retirement. Was this comparable? Not really—I liked accounting (believe it or not). And I really liked the idea of being paid well as soon as

I had a diploma in hand. But something about it just felt . . . wrong.

"I think I want to go to law school," I said.

Her eyes widened slightly.

"Have you applied?"

"Yes, ma'am."

"Do you mind if I ask where?"

I ticked off the list that had been casually assembled, with little input from any outside source (there was no one to help guide me through the process): Seton Hall, Temple, University of Baltimore, Hofstra (of course) . . . and Georgetown.

"Georgetown?" she repeated. "Have you heard back yet?"

I said that I had not heard anything; it was early still.

And then she did something extraordinary. Well, two things, actually.

First, she told me that if I wanted to go to law school, then that's what I should do.

"We'd love to have you at Arthur Andersen, but you should trust your instincts."

"I could defer acceptance," I suggested. "Maybe work for a few years and then go to school."

She smiled. "Yes, you could. But speaking from experience, that probably won't happen. If you take the money, you'll like the money. And then every year there will be a little more of it, and you'll get older, and after a while you'll forget that you ever wanted to go to law school."

"Oh . . . Is that a bad thing?"

"I can't answer that for you."

Another long pause.

"What's your dream school?" she asked.

"Georgetown, I suppose." I said this only because it was the most competitive school on my application list. I hadn't applied to any of the Ivies, figuring they were out of my reach, both financially and competitively. Whether this was true or not, I didn't know, but it felt that way. Georgetown was my "reach" school.

"Do you have any contacts there?" she asked.

I laughed. "No."

"Well, I do."

That was the second extraordinary thing. Instead of packing her briefcase and walking away and telling me what a fool I was for turning down a great job, she not only encouraged me to follow my dream, she also reached out to a colleague who could help make that dream come true. There was no reason for her to do this; she had absolutely nothing to gain. But she did it anyway, perhaps because she was simply a good person, or perhaps it had something to do with our shared experience (although I didn't know anything about her background, aside from the obvious, which is that she was Black).

She gave me the name of a man who worked in undergraduate student affairs at Georgetown, primarily with minority students. He had nothing to do with the law school, but he could, if so inclined, act as a conduit. We talked on the phone, hit it off, and he set up a meeting with Ted Miller, who was the director of admissions at Georgetown University Law Center. That was the chain of events, beyond my control, that helped lead to my application getting a comprehensive review at Georgetown. I still had to get in on my own merit, on the strength of my academic record, but that interview certainly allowed me to strengthen my case and contributed to my acceptance. I was no longer just a name and a number on an application. I was a person they had taken the time to meet and interview. And it all began with a recruiter for Arthur Andersen having the decency and compassion to look beyond her own self-interests.

A newly minted college graduate might technically be a legal adult, but I was still feeling the weight of adolescent insecurity. A smart and assured mentor or adviser—or just a wise and honest stranger—can make such a big difference at that stage of life. For me, one of those people was a Hofstra business law professor named Leslie Geller. A Harvard-trained lawyer in his sixties, Professor Geller loved teaching; he also loved talking about the law. I took two of his classes at Hofstra, did well in both, and over time, we developed a strong relationship. Although Professor Geller was white, he had a deep and abiding interest in the inequities and lack of opportunities for African Americans in the legal profession.

"I think you could be a very good attorney," he had told me on more than one occasion, an endorsement that carried weight and pushed me away from the cocoon of accounting and toward the uncertainty of law school.

There were money issues. As usual. I didn't have the resources to attend Georgetown, and even if I maxed out student loans, I'd still fall short. An avenue of possibility presented itself in the form of the Council on Legal Education Opportunity (CLEO) program, which was similar in spirit to the NOAH program at Hofstra. I spent the summer after graduation at Dickinson College in Pennsylvania, taking classes and jockeying for scholarship money with other prelaw students. I did well in most of the summer classes but struggled in one, which prompted a white professor to pull me aside and question whether there had been some mistake.

"Maybe," he suggested, "you're just not up to this."

I realized that it would never stop, that some people would forever judge me based on the color of my skin and the fact that I was a poor city kid. I couldn't do anything about that. But I could prove them wrong. Just as in college, I would outwork everyone (or almost everyone). And, just as in college, I would take advantage of fortune. I would embrace the words and actions of those willing to lend a hand on the way up and out of my conditions. Those kind enough to take a breath and say, "We believe in you. We know you can do this." I vowed to pay those gifts back one day with my own time and energy. To keep the ball moving forward for others like me.

But in my excitement, I had overlooked some of the details of my next step to Georgetown. A month before the start of classes, having finished the CLEO program and received a modest package of scholarships and loans, I began to have second thoughts. As an accounting major, I was somewhat obsessed with facts and figures, with putting numbers on each side of the ledger and assessing the likelihood of a positive outcome. What I saw was this: I would graduate from Georgetown with a debt so immense that it seemed almost unfathomable. Ten years down the road, I'd be in my midthirties and still paying back student loans.

One day I found myself in the throes of a panic attack.

Why had I turned down that job at Arthur Andersen? What was I thinking? What arrogance and stupidity had brought me to this place?

I decided at the last second to put in an application at Brooklyn School of Law. The tuition was significantly less than Georgetown, there might be more scholarship money available, and I could live at home or with relatives in Brooklyn. If I got a part-time job, I could conceivably come out of law school debt-free. Given that I was months late in the application process, I had to quickly schedule a meeting with the dean of the law school (which was granted only because my grades were so strong). I apologized for my tardiness and explained my financial situation.

We chatted for a while, and the dean looked over my transcript. He told me that even though I had missed the deadline for application, they would grant admission. However, there was no scholarship money available beyond what the CLEO program had awarded; next year, perhaps. But I didn't care. No matter how I crunched the numbers, Brooklyn would be far less expensive. Whether the prospect of relocating factored into the equation, I can't say for sure. On some level, it probably did. Washington, DC, was only a couple hundred miles away, but it seemed so much farther. New York was home. New York, I knew.

I was ready to accept the offer when the dean did something completely unexpected. Just like the recruiter from Arthur Andersen, he challenged me, forced me to question my own motives and decisions.

"Look, I think you'd do well here, and we'd be happy to give you a spot. You're obviously a strong student. But I have to tell you this: If you got into Georgetown, that's where you should go. Not many students have that opportunity."

I told him I understood, but that the cost was prohibitive. He was a white man with a prestigious job—I did not expect him to understand where I was coming from. But, again, maybe he saw something in me that I did not see in myself.

"It is expensive," he said. "But whatever you have to borrow, you should borrow it, because with a degree from Georgetown, you will have no trouble paying it back."

He paused, smiled.

"Might take a while, but in the long run, you will have significantly more earning power."

"So . . . you don't think I should come here?"

"I just don't want to see you make a mistake that you might regret for the rest of your life."

———————————

If Hofstra was my first taste of culture shock, Georgetown was like a five-course meal. There were six hundred students in my first-year class. Ten percent were students of color, which made Georgetown one of the more diverse populations among the nation's top law schools, but I soon discovered that even among students of color, I was an outlier. It is one thing to be a Black student in a predominantly white environment. It is quite another to be a Black student from the projects. There weren't a lot of other first-generation college graduates at Georgetown. In fact, sometimes it felt like I was one of the few people in my class who didn't come from a long line of lawyers, some of whom were intimidatingly successful. I had one classmate whose grandfather was a Supreme Court justice! He was a nice-enough kid, but it was hard to feel like we had anything in common. I couldn't imagine what Christmas must have been like at his house growing up, and I'm sure he couldn't have imagined what it was like at mine.

In my first year, I lived with Johan, a fraternity brother from Hofstra who was attending law school at George Washington University. The following year, a fraternity brother named Cliff, who had graduated from Adelphi, also enrolled at GW. Those two, along with a classmate at Georgetown named David Green, whose background was not dissimilar from my own, became my closest friends. David was the Bronx kid I mentioned earlier—he went to Amherst High School in central Massachusetts, a product of one of those programs that sent inner-city students to suburban high schools or boarding schools for a leg up. He had obtained his undergraduate degree from Georgetown, knew DC, and knew the Georgetown campus like an old pro. Socially, academically, and philosophically, he was a friend and guiding light.

"Hang in there, Bruce," he'd say if I was having a tough time. "We can reach the stars."

I was making a home in DC, but the struggle continued. In the summer after my first year of law school I told my mother that I didn't know if I'd be able to return to Georgetown the following year. The rent for my share of the apartment, combined with tuition, was simply more than I could afford. She reached out to my great-aunt Zeola, who lived in New York, and asked if she might be willing to contact her DC-based sister, Ceola. I know this is confusing, with the branches of the family tree becoming hopelessly entangled—my mother soliciting help from my father's aunt (Ceola), whom my father apparently did not even know. I barely understood it myself at the time.

Regardless, I wound up living with Aunt Ceola for the last two years of law school. She suffered from glaucoma and as a result was nearly blind, but she could cook up a storm, nonetheless. Everything in the kitchen was in a designated spot, moved only for cooking and cleaning, and then returned to its proper place. To witness her craft was a remarkable thing, the way she moved assuredly around the kitchen, her hands gliding across the pots and pans and utensils, lighting burners, and adjusting the heat using only her sense of touch. She never burned herself and rarely spilled so much as a drop. But her power did not stop there.

I'd come home at midnight after a long night in the library, and she'd be waiting up for me with some food and a smile. Then, she'd walk over to a piano she kept in the house and tap the bench.

"Sit down, Junior. Let's play."

I was far from a great pianist, but I had learned to play a little in high school, and I could read music and fumble my way across the keys well enough to sound like I knew what I was doing. That was sufficient to make Aunt Ceola happy. She'd sing while I played—gospel songs like "Jesus Loves Me," religious standards, Christmas carols during the holidays. I did that virtually every night for two years. You could say I literally sang for my supper.

In law school, as in college, my choice of classes challenged assumptions. Most of my peers avoided tax law, deeming it boring or unglamorous. I took six classes in tax law at Georgetown and did well in all of them. In my second year, a Caucasian professor named Patricia White, apparently surprised by my aptitude, asked if I had taken the class previously.

Here we go again.

When I responded that I had not, she smiled and suggested that I might be a candidate for a particular summer internship. I thanked her, applied for the job, and, with her recommendation, got it.

Whatever preconceived notions Professor White might have had toward me—and I toward her—they melted away as we got to know each other. First of all, she was an extraordinary teacher who had a rare gift not just for making complicated material accessible but also for making tax law seem exciting! Second, and perhaps more important, she was a mentor—someone who encouraged promising students and helped facilitate their career ambitions through internships and recommendations, sometimes long after graduation.

Professor White went on to join the faculty at her alma mater, the University of Michigan Law School, before becoming the dean of Arizona State University College of Law and, later, Miami University School of Law. She was a trailblazer, and I am proud to count her as a friend and colleague to this day.

The internship was at Silverstein and Mullens, an old and esteemed DC law firm specializing in tax work. I was the first Black summer associate (or attorney, for that matter) the firm had ever hired. In general, people were nice enough, but my status as an outsider—a curiosity—was cemented one day during a luncheon at the über-elite George Town Club, attended by the summer associates and hosted by the founding partner himself, Mr. Leonard Silverstein, along with some other partners and associates. At some point in this extremely uncomfortable setting, the conversation turned to matters of social justice and inequity and other lofty issues unsolvable over lunch at the pristine George Town Club. I overheard someone use the word *ghetto*. Suddenly, there was a pause in the conversation as Mr. Silverstein turned to me.

I didn't know much about Leonard Silverstein beyond his résumé, which was appropriately impressive: Harvard educated, helped shape the modern-day Internal Revenue Code, noted philanthropist who sat on the President's Committee on the Arts and Humanities. He was in his midsixties at the time and still an active and weighty presence both at the firm and in DC legal circles. But those are just things you hear and read, stuff that ends up in the first paragraph of an obituary. It's a public persona shaped by the stuff you do when people are watching. I did not know Leonard Silverstein as a person . . . as a man. For obvious reasons—I was a lowly summer associate; he was the founder of the company—our lives did not intersect. Until this very moment, not a word had ever passed between us.

"Young man," he said, smiling in a way that was probably meant to be paternal, but came off as something else. "You probably know more about the ghetto than anyone else here. Maybe you can help us out?"

He said this without a trace of emotion. It wasn't meant to be demeaning or humorous. It was said with utter sincerity . . .

and cluelessness. It was, in some ways, the worst sort of racism, the kind based not on hatred but on assumptions and ignorance. I looked around the table, which had fallen completely silent. Some of the younger associates were visibly uncomfortable, while some of the older partners were curious to hear my response, as if Mr. Silverstein had asked a perfectly reasonable question.

Here, it seemed, was the emperor devoid of clothing.

I thought long and hard before speaking. The money I made that summer was more money than I had ever seen, but I'd gotten by without it most of my life, and if it suddenly disappeared, I wouldn't miss it. What I decided, ultimately, was that my dignity was more important than any job.

"With all due respect, sir . . . you don't know me," I began. "You don't even know my name. You don't know where I'm from or anything about me. What do you mean, I should know about the ghetto? In fact, I don't know anything about the ghetto. What do you know, sir?"

The reaction in the dining room fell somewhere between abject horror and embarrassment, as utensils hovered in midair, uncommitted, and my voice began to rise.

"Perhaps you can educate me about the ghetto, because that's not where I'm from. I'd like to hear what you know, sir."

Now, obviously, this was not entirely true. I knew my way around the ghetto. I had grown up in the projects, and I had lived in some very bad areas in Brooklyn. That wasn't the point. The point was, someone who had power and authority and wealth—Ivy-draped Leonard Silverstein (Yale undergrad, in addition to Harvard Law), scion of a Washington, DC, law firm—assumed, based simply on the color of my skin, that *I* was a product of the ghetto. Whether his assumption was correct or incorrect did not matter in the least.

The luncheon broke up minutes after I finished speaking. There were no apologies or cordial goodbyes. By the time I got back to the office, wondering if I would be asked to clean out my desk, word had already gotten around. A few partners who weren't at the luncheon offered their apologies, perhaps less out of genuine compassion than concern that I would report to Georgetown Law School that a deep strain of racism ran through the marrow of Silverstein and Mullens, thus souring the firm's reputation among potential recruits.

I did not lose my job. In fact, upon graduation, I was offered a position with Silverstein and Mullens, which understandably provoked ambivalence.

"Come on, Bruce," my friend Cliff had said when I told him of the offer. "You don't want to work for those assholes."

He was right—I didn't want to work for those assholes. But I also knew that Silverstein and Mullens was no different from any other prestigious, stately law firm, founded by folks whose ancestors crossed the Atlantic on the *Mayflower*. There were assholes, and racists, everywhere in the upper realm of the legal profession, but there were good people, too. If I wanted to work at that level, and perhaps have an opportunity to change the system . . . to one day open doors for others . . . then I'd have to try to work from within.

"You know what?" I said to Cliff, "I know who this guy [Silverstein] is. I'd rather work at a place where I understand what I'm dealing with than someplace where people are lying and hiding who they are."

It wasn't easy. The firm had no Black attorneys, so I spent a lot of my free time with the people who worked in the cafeteria or the mailroom, talking with them, bonding. None of the other attorneys did this, of course. And I didn't do it out of some noble gesture; I did it because I was lonely and isolated, and sometimes I just needed to spend time with people whose backgrounds were not so different from my own. This included Mr. Silverstein's personal driver, a Black man who laughed when I told him the luncheon story.

"You're not surprised?" I asked.

He shook his head. "Not at all. Dude's an old-school racist. Probably doesn't even know he did anything wrong."

Sometimes Mr. Silverstein would see me in the library and get this curious look on his face. Then, he'd walk over and strike up an awkward, almost accusatory conversation. There was one time I was doing research on tax codes. For me, or any student well versed in tax law, it was simple and formulaic. You look up the code, and if you need further information, you research the legislative intent behind the code. Mr. Silverstein hovered over me while I went through this process, a look of bemusement on his face.

"How do you know how to do this?" he asked.

I sighed, tried to maintain my composure.

"Sir, I took six classes in tax at Georgetown. This is pretty basic stuff." I paused. "But I can show you how to do it, if you'd like."

Mr. Silverstein stared at me. With the thinnest of smiles, he nodded, said nothing, and walked away.

As a second-year associate at Silverstein and Mullens, I was on a stratospheric trajectory, making approximately seventy grand a year in 1990 dollars (new associates at top law firms in 2022 are making close to $200,000)—comparable to the top associate pay at any firm in the country. I pooled resources with my friend David Green, who had taken a job as a federal judicial clerk, and together we purchased a three-bedroom town house on Capitol Hill. This was a nice place to live, but it was also an investment opportunity.

While I liked the money and the security that came with it, I was unhappy and unsure of what I wanted to do with my life—a condition exacerbated by an evolving relationship with a former college girlfriend that included a pregnancy for which, she said, I was responsible. I disputed her claim, and a paternity test eventually confirmed that I could not have been the father. But that is merely the beginning—or perhaps the midpoint—of a long and winding road. Despite this fractious event, our relationship endured. We ended up moving in together, and I took care of the child, a lovely girl named Jenell, as if she were my own. We had two more children, Maya and Sabree. We separated. Life went on.

But I'm getting ahead of myself.

I wanted to be a trailblazer at Silverstein and Mullens—the first Black attorney ever hired at the firm—but I don't know that I really understood what that entailed, or that I would choose to do it again. The long hours sitting alone at a desk, poring over documents, working through lunch not merely because you're swamped but because no one has invited you to join their group. Sounds a bit like middle school, I realize, but that's the reality of being the only Black attorney at an otherwise all-white firm. I don't think any of it was malicious, or even intentional. It was just business as usual. But for me, it was yet another indignity to overcome each day.

I had two entirely separate lives: one within the walls of Silverstein and Mullens, the other outside. I had a busy social life and interests beyond the firm, including a fledgling talent-management company that I had started with a couple fraternity brothers from Hofstra and the pursuit of a master's of law in taxation at Georgetown. I was busier than I ever thought possible, but I loved the frantic nature of it all, fed off the rush to fill every waking moment with something meaningful, something measurable, something to chart the distance between where I had started and where I was going. It wasn't enough to have a good job and a fat paycheck. Progress was required, quantifiable proof that I wasn't stagnating or settling; that there was no chance I'd ever slip back to the life I'd left behind; that the sacrifices made on my behalf, and the confidence bestowed upon me by my mother and grandmother and my aunt—and by so many other people—was warranted. And that the doubters—from the principal who held me back in fourth grade all the way up to Leonard Silverstein—were wrong.

Stop and smell the roses? I didn't even notice they'd been planted.

After two years, I negotiated a separation agreement with Silverstein and Mullens. I had signed on with the understanding that the job would lead to a partnership track, but I was no longer interested in working there, let alone becoming a partner. The agreement allowed for a scaling back of responsibility, which in turn allowed me to spend one semester studying full-time for my master's degree.

Around this same time, I attended the annual Black Entertainment and Sports Lawyers Association conference in Jamaica, ostensibly to make contacts in the field that I hoped might help advance the cause of our little talent-management company, but also to explore other opportunities outside the realm of tax law. There I was introduced to a woman named Denise Brown, a partner with the Manhattan firm of Minter and Gay, a small but increasingly influential entity in the world of entertainment, sports, and labor law. Kendall Minter was still in his thirties at the time but already had acquired the sort of résumé and client list (jazz legends Lena Horne and Cassandra Wilson; R&B stalwarts Cameo, Freddie Jackson, and Teddy Riley; funk stars Kool & the Gang; rappers the Fat Boys and Heavy D & the Boyz; and Reggae star Peter Tosh, just to name a few) that made every young attorney in the entertainment field—or at least every young Black attorney— want to work with him.

And now I was one of the lucky few being pulled into his orbit.

"You should come and work for us," Denise said. "You'll love it. Kendall is a genius."

"So I've heard. I've also heard you don't pay very well."

This was true. Minter and Gay was a boutique agency, with Kendall as the star and a cadre of associates supporting the effort in exchange for what would really be an intense but highly valuable, glorified internship. (Denise had passed through this crucible herself, on the way to becoming a partner.) But if I was serious about making the jump from tax law to entertainment law—a move that could, perhaps, facilitate the commingling of the passions of my youth (art, theater, movies, music) with the training of my adulthood—then an alignment with Kendall Minter was a bold step backward in the hope of soon taking two giant steps forward.

"Money isn't everything," Denise said with a shrug.

Easy for you to say, I thought. Denise had worked on Wall Street prior to joining Minter and Gay, where, among other notable achievements, she had assisted Reginald Lewis and the TLC Group in a $1.2 billion acquisition of Beatrice International.

"Yeah, but a man's gotta eat."

We both laughed. And I knew what she was thinking: *Sometimes it's better to be hungry.*

Chapter 10

PETE ROCK & CL SMOOTH

Whoever said "You can't go home again" probably never took an 80 percent pay cut while simultaneously trying to relocate to one of the most expensive cities in the world.

I accepted the offer from Minter and Gay shortly after completing graduate studies at Georgetown. The compensation package did not carry a specific dollar value. It would be based somewhat nebulously on a percentage of work that I brought into the firm. But I knew it wouldn't be much—that was an understood part of the arrangement: labor in exchange for education and experience and contacts. (Over the course of two years, I earned approximately $12,000.) I'll admit to swallowing hard before closing that deal and subsequently enduring a few restless nights. In my heart, I knew it was the right decision. I wanted to practice entertainment law, and Kendall Minter was among the best in the business. But his office was located in Lower Manhattan, and there was absolutely no chance that I could survive exclusively on the deal his firm was offering. Not in New York. Maybe not anywhere.

"Don't worry," Denise Brown had told me. "You'll figure it out."

She was right. If I wanted to work with Kendall, I'd have to get creative. I'd also have to work harder than I ever thought possible, because a second job would be necessary in order to make ends meet—or at least bring the threads closer together. Given that I'd be working fifty to sixty hours a week at Minter and Gay, there weren't a lot of outside options. There was one possibility, however: teaching. Academia allowed for some flexibility—with evening classes, movable office hours, and prep time whenever I could squeeze it in.

I submitted résumés to several colleges and universities in the metropolitan area, got a few interviews, and ultimately landed an offer to teach at Baruch College. Like most non-tenure track jobs in higher education, the salary was not great, but combined with the income from Minter and Gay, it at least qualified as a living wage. Still not nearly what I would have earned as a third-year associate at Silverstein and Mullens (or any other top law firm), but that was okay. The goal was long-term development, not short-term comfort.

With that in mind, I called my mother and informed her of my plans. At first, I'm not sure she understood. Why, she wondered, would I give up a lucrative job for what seemed to be nothing more than an internship?

"You'd make more than that at Chase," she said incredulously.

"Yeah, Mommy, I know. I'm going teach at Baruch as well. I'll be fine. Trust me."

"Okay. Is there anything I can do to help?"

I hesitated. There was, in fact, one thing she could do.

"What would you think about me coming home to live with you?"

"In the projects?" She laughed. "I'm not going anywhere. You're always welcome here. You know that."

I did know. I'd been home many times to visit in the previous half dozen years, had spent a lot of time with family and friends in both Manhattan and Brooklyn. Home was home: warm, loving, always there if you needed it. But never did I think I might actually move back into my mother's apartment, full-time. It was almost too strange to consider. I had a degree from one of the top law schools in the country. I had spent two years on the track to partner at a prestigious DC firm. And now I was chucking it all to return to the Amsterdam Houses?

I suppose some people would have viewed this as a failure. I saw it as a compromise—a perfectly reasonable and practical solution to a complex problem. Living in the projects afforded me the opportunity to do the type of work that I really wanted to do, without going even deeper in debt to make it happen. Between the two jobs, I'd be working seven days a week, sunup to sundown. Not having to worry about rent, a mortgage, or even food (since there was always plenty in the house) was a blessing.

In some ways, I might have been a bit naive, thinking I could easily slip back into the housing project on Amsterdam Avenue—back to the very same apartment where I had been raised and where my mother still lived—without experiencing any sort of cognitive dissonance. I stayed there for more than two years, with one foot in the fast-paced, glittery world of entertainment law, and one foot in the past—in a world punctuated by poverty and drugs and violence and crime.

Within the first two weeks of returning home, I became graphically reacquainted with the reality of my old neighborhood. I left the apartment one day in a bit of a rush, so rather than waiting for the elevator, I entered the stairwell and began my descent. A couple floors down, I passed a skittish young man with sunken eyes. As I went by, he called out.

"Hey!"

I turned around, saw him flash a gun.

"Against the wall!"

It occurred to me as he put the gun against my face that a lot of time had passed since I'd lived in the projects. I had no idea who this kid was, and he did not know me. Whatever protection my reputation had once afforded, it was now gone. And yet, I still had a few cards to play. I realized that just beyond the stairwell door was an apartment belonging to a friend of mine named James. He was a drug dealer when I left town, and he was still a drug dealer. It made sense that this kid was either working for James or was coming after James. He seemed too young and twitchy to go after a big dog like James, so I gambled that he was merely hired help.

"You know James?" I said, trying to remain calm.

He stiffened, held the gun securely. "What's it to you?"

"That's my brother," I said, speaking metaphorically. "We go back."

The kid lowered the gun, took a step in reverse. He opened the door to the hallway and yelled, "Hey, James!"

Nothing.

Again. "HEY, JAMES!"

This time James emerged. He motioned us into the hall-way and smiled at me. Then he gave the kid a look of admonishment.

"The fuck you doing, man? That's Bruce."

"Bruce who?"

"He's family," James said. "Back the fuck off."

Now the kid was flustered, embarrassed. "Sorry. I didn't know."

He disappeared. James shook his head, laughed, and threw an arm around me.

"Yo, man, you've been away too long. Watch your step. These kids don't know you, and some of them are . . . reckless."

I nodded. "Understood. Thanks."

Interestingly, this dichotomy—Georgetown-trained attorney living in his old home in the projects—proved beneficial when I began working with clients in the music industry, predominantly African American rappers, hip hop artists and producers from New York whose backgrounds were not dissimilar from my own. Artists like Tony Dofat, Trackmasters, and Pete Rock & CL Smooth. These guys all needed lawyers who would look out for them and help them make solid business decisions while hopefully protecting their money, and the fact was, there were few African American entertainment lawyers in those days, and even fewer who had risen from the street.

But I could look them in the eye and tell them that I understood how they felt—their allegiance to friends and family (even if some of those people were involved in illicit activity); their tendency to be distrustful of the ancient hier-archy that ruled the entertainment world, and of white institutions in general. I would be straight with them and would work to protect them. I was not a slick Manhattan lawyer, eager to get in their pockets. I was one of them.

More important, since so many of these artists were young—basically kids—I could tell their mothers and grandmothers the same thing. Fathers were less likely to be present, but when they were, they tended to be deeply invested and concerned.

Such was the case with Pete Rock, who was one of the top producers on the East Coast, but who was also embroiled in a contract dispute around the time I went to his home to discuss representation. The pitch was not just to him but to his entire family. I got it. I understood their concerns, their fear, their mistrust. The music business has always been brutal and unforgiving, known for eating its young. Guileless, eager artists, regardless of ethnic background, have long been easy targets. But Black artists in the music industry, particularly in the early days of rap and hip hop, often signed onerous contracts that left them with only a fraction of the profits from their art and labor. Whatever money they did make seemed to slip through their fingers, since they had no one to provide sound financial advice. The artist's career, like the professional athlete's career, is often fleeting. Every penny should be counted and invested wisely.

"I'll help you do that," I said.

Their pitch to me was simple, profound, and from the heart.

"I didn't raise my son to become successful and then turn him over to a white man," Pete Rock's father said flatly. "So, we're going to trust you. Please take care of him."

"Yes, sir," I said as we shook hands to close the deal.

Signing Pete Rock was a watershed moment for my career, my first big "get" for Minter and Gay. I'd been with the firm almost two years by that point, and it had been every bit as positive and exhausting as I'd hoped it would be. Through both Kendall and Denise, I gained access to the inner workings of the entertainment industry—specifically, how contracts and deals were structured. Unlike my previous position, I received invaluable training and mentorship. I had come to New York in hope of receiving the equivalent of a graduate degree in entertainment law, and that's exactly what I got.

But, as with any graduate program (or internship), the arrangement had a natural life span. It was never presented as a partner-track position; I was there to learn and to work, and to soak up as much knowledge as I could, while also helping Kendall and Denise expand their practice. I knew from the first day I walked into the office that eventually I'd be moving on. This was perfectly fine, and we all entered into the agreement with complete transparency.

Kendall could not have been more supportive—he even encouraged me to begin developing my own practice while I was still working for him. By the second year, I had accrued enough experience and contacts that talent was beginning to come to me specifically, as opposed to the firm. Kendall was fine with that, so long as I included the firm in any deals that were made while I worked for him. But it was inevitable that I would leave and strike out on my own. The trick was in determining when the time was right to do that.

As it turned out, signing Pete Rock was the inciting incident.

I mentioned that Pete was unhappy with his contract and that I helped him get out of it, but that is a gross simplification of the process. There were multiple steps along the way, each of which tested not just my knowledge of contracts and the law but also my ability to sell and to negotiate; to do battle with adversaries in a calm and professional manner. I had been trained as a tax attorney, which by definition meant that I was accustomed to working in a quiet and reserved corner of the legal profession. Entertainment attorneys, on the other hand, tend to be fighters. The entertainment attorney is like an accountant, agent, and manager, all rolled into one. A one-man (or -woman) army enlisted with the sole objective to get the best possible deal for a client.

I had been introduced to Pete Rock & CL Smooth by Erskine Isaac, a fraternity brother of mine from Hofstra who was also part of the management company we had started. That company had long since fizzled out, and while I had moved on to tax law and then entertainment law, Erskine was in the process of developing a successful booking agency (a booker serves as an intermediary between artists and the venues at which they perform). Among his clients were Pete Rock & CL Smooth, who by the early 1990s had become mainstays of the East Coast rap and hip hop scene. They started out performing as a duo, with CL on vocals and Pete handling the production and DJ responsibilities. By this time, though, Pete's career and reputation were in ascendance. He and Dr. Dre were the top two producers in hip hop—and you could have made a compelling case that Dre was number two.

Although still only in his early twenties, Pete was one of the most gifted and creative forces in music; everyone wanted to work with him. Unfortunately, as often happens in the entertainment business, Pete was locked into an unfavorable contract that predated his rising celebrity. And now he wanted out. Specifically, he and CL wanted to sever ties with Untouchables Entertainment Group, the management company and record label founded by Edward "DJ Eddie F" Ferrell, a multitalented hyphenate (rapper-producer-executive) who, like Pete, was a native of Mount Vernon, New York.

This was sticky stuff, with personal relationships, career trajectories, artistic integrity, and a boatload of money at stake. Part of the problem was that, like so many musical artists throughout history, Pete and Eddie F were just kids who suddenly found fame and fortune, and while the success was certainly welcome, it did not come without baggage. Pete wanted the freedom to work with other artists and to negotiate deals reflective of his newfound status. Untouchables Entertainment wanted to protect their investment.

There was nothing nefarious or malicious on either side of the argument. What there was, I hoped to prove, was a degree of inexperience that led to poor administration and a lack of funds flowing in the proper direction. In short, Untouchables Entertainment owed money to Pete Rock & CL Smooth, and in my opinion this debt represented a breach of contract. Really, though, money was tangential to the equation. The goal was to break the contract, thus allowing Pete to pursue whatever artistic and commercial opportunities might be available for someone in his creative prime. Sure, money had to change hands, and in the end, at least in terms of the settlement, most of that money flowed in what might appear to be the wrong direction: from Pete Rock to

Untouchables Entertainment. But that's missing the point. We made our case that Pete's contract was not enforceable and thus pushed Untouchables into a buyout. They would receive a certain amount of money in exchange for releasing Pete from his contract. This was exactly what we had hoped to accomplish. As a musical artist and producer, Pete Rock was the equivalent of a free agent, able to negotiate with all bidders. And like a basketball player who had just made the all-star team, he had tremendous leverage.

As Pete's performing and recording partner, CL Smooth was part of the deal, but Pete was perceived as the more coveted entity. His skill as a producer, writer, and DJ made him a rare talent, one sought out by other rappers and hip hop artists interested in collaboration. Then, as now, vocalists were not the stars of the burgeoning hip hop universe. Producers drove the machinery—creatively and financially.

Naturally, just about every record label wanted to enter into a production deal with Pete Rock, figuring not only would he work with artists already signed to their label, but he'd also attract new talent. Everything was a little more complicated with a Pete Rock deal because he also wanted to continue making his own records, which meant subdividing his contract into sections devoted to various responsibilities and opportunities as both a producer and performer (record labels preferred narrow categorizations and clearly defined roles). But when someone is as talented as Pete, you find a way to make it work.

Complicating matters significantly was the fact that Pete and CL Smooth also had a recording deal with Elektra Records. Even though the recording deal had been negotiated by

Untouchables Entertainment, and their contract with Untouchables had been dissolved, the partnership with Elektra remained in place. There was no way to prove breach of contract against Elektra because, frankly, there was none. But Elektra wanted to make a long-term investment in Pete and CL, and the only way to do that was for Elektra to keep them happy, so they agreed to renegotiate the recording contract. After that, we were free to negotiate with anyone who wanted to sign Pete to a production deal, which was pretty much every label in the music industry. In the end, Elektra outbid everyone to ensure exclusive access to Pete and his expanding orbit of artists.

This was difficult, sometimes nasty business, and the more I saw, the more I came to believe that unethical behavior was commonplace in the entertainment industry. Not necessarily with Elektra, specifically, but there were executives (usually white and covered with the dust of decades spent in the same office) so desperate to sign the top rap and hip hop clients (at a time when those genres were beginning to dominate the airwaves and album sales) that they would offer up deals with their rock musicians as a sort of quid pro quo.

"Give us Pete Rock and we'll make sure we steer (*fill in the name of almost any white rock musician of the 1990s*) to your firm."

To which I would reply, "Do you really think I'd sell out my guys? Fuck you."

Like I said, nasty business. It was also, I must admit, thrilling.

I loved fighting for my clients, tracing every penny across reams of frequently indecipherable accounting records: bank statements, receipts, 1099 forms, expenditures, transcripts, and pay stubs. I loved taking a yellow highlighter to a fifty-page contract and marking each and every flaw. This was what I had worked for; this was the result of a decade of college and law school and training. I felt . . . unleashed.

I was still almost a kid myself at the time, not yet thirty years old, but I felt a paternal obligation toward my clients, so many of whom were young and gifted, and loaded with street smarts, but impulsive and unwise in the ways of the corporate world. It's no secret that the East Coast versus West Coast rap battles of the 1990s involved some heavy criminal and gang influence, but it's also true that artists of the era were primarily Black and thus more likely to be treated harshly by the criminal justice system. They needed legal support on a number of levels.

In 1993, after a few years with Minter and Gay, I moved to the Bronx and became a founding member of the New York law firm Jackson, Brown, Powell, and St. George, started with some fraternity brothers and a friend from law school. We were primarily an entertainment firm but also had a small component devoted to criminal matters.

The early years were lean but exciting; the transition to self-employment—to entrepreneurship—at once exhausting and exhilarating. Pete Rock & CL Smooth came with me when I hung out my shingle, and their presence on the client list gave us instant credibility and access to record company executives and other artists who not only took our calls but also, in many cases, did the calling.

We'd been in business only a few months when Russell Simmons reached out. Russell was a titan of hip hop at the time, the cofounder, along with Rick Rubin, of Def Jam

Recordings. Like everyone else, he was interested in working with Pete Rock, and to do that, he had to go through our little firm. We had only recently moved into a small office space at 230 Park Avenue that included a conference room for meetings. Russell suggested, however, that we meet for lunch at a restaurant in the West Village.

None of us had cars at the time—we simply couldn't afford them. Instead, we traveled around the city on foot, or by bus, cab, or subway. No big deal; that's the way a lot of people get around New York. On the rare occasion when we had to travel together, we'd borrow a car that belonged to my partner Cliff Brown's grandmother: a '70s-era Dodge Dart that was pockmarked with rust but got decent gas mileage and could be crammed into the tiniest of parking spots. Alas, the doors worked only sporadically, so as often as not, you had to roll down the window and climb out, leaving the car open to thieves and vandals, neither of which ever seemed to take much of an interest.

It wasn't the kind of vehicle that screamed *Power!* But it got the job done. Eventually, we'd all get BMWs, both to present an image of prosperity and success and because we could afford to do it, but you only eat what you can kill, as they say, and for the better part of two years, that little Dodge was our only mode of private transportation.

We met at the office and drove to the restaurant, then spent ten minutes driving around the neighborhood looking for a parking space that was close enough to walk, but not so close that we'd be seen getting into the car after the meeting. We all wore dark, conservative suits. On this point there was no debate. The artists we represented were often kids in street wear or adults in flashy outfits of questionable taste. Our sartorial approach, agreed upon in a staff meeting, would be decidedly different. We were professionals . . . attorneys. We did quiet, serious work in a field sometimes known for bombast. You might not mind if your sound engineer was wearing a red leather jacket and parachute pants, but you really didn't want your attorney (or your accountant) to dress that way.

You wanted your attorney to be the smartest, most humorless guy in the room. You wanted him to be equal parts bean counter and assassin. And you wanted him to look the part. Especially when dealing with someone like Russell Simmons, who had long since passed the point of needing to prove anything to anyone. A lot of people in the entertainment business, including entertainment attorneys, tried to look slick and cool. I decided very early on that I would leave slick and cool to the artists. I had a JD and master's of law (LLM) from Georgetown, and I wanted to present an image that reflected the work and intelligence that went into acquiring those letters behind my name. I wouldn't exactly call it a strategy; it was more of a philosophy. But it instantly separated us from most of our peers.

There was very little talk of actual business at the restaurant, which came as something of a surprise. Russell wanted to get to know us and our firm. He wanted to know a little bit about our personal lives—our families, our backgrounds. Where had we grown up, gone to school? Why had we chosen the legal profession? What sort of music did we like (apart from Pete Rock, of course)?

After lunch, Russell suggested we go to his apartment to continue the discussion. He lived just a few blocks away, which was fortuitous, because we could all walk rather than try to extricate the car from its parking spot and then drive to another part of town, find a new parking spot sufficiently far away to avoid our being noticed (and discovered as shit-box-driving frauds), and approach on foot. Pete was not present for either the lunch or the meeting, so Russell asked a lot of questions about how we had come to manage him and what sort of vision we had for his future.

I suppose a part of me expected Russell to be condescending or arrogant in that meeting, but he proved to be exactly the opposite: polite, professional, inquisitive in a charming sort of way. What I learned that day is that power is based not just on a résumé or awards, or even on how much money you have in your bank account. (Or what type of car you drive!) It is based on commodities, talent being the rarest and most important. By any reasonable measure, Russell and I were not on even footing. Although he was only five years older than I was, Russell was already a certified media mogul. He was wealthy; I was . . . not. He was a household name; I was a name only in my own household.

But I had Pete Rock, one of the more precious commodities in hip hop. And with that commodity came power. Everyone wanted access to Pete, and I was the gatekeeper. As the conversation with Russell went on, I felt increasingly empowered.

Hmmmmm . . . I'm not trying to sell you; you're trying to sell me.

Russell, of course, was a step ahead of us. He'd been down this road before and knew precisely how to comport himself. There wasn't an opportunity in that meeting for him to be anything but gracious, so that's exactly the way he behaved. He offered flattering assessments of Pete's talent as both producer and performer and served up a casual over-view of his artistic vision if they were to work together under the Def Jam label. It was low-key, professional, appropriate.

I learned something else from that meeting (and from similar, subsequent meetings): when you are the gatekeeper, it's tempting—but unwise—to let your ego run wild. Pete Rock was the magnet that initially attracted a roster of talent to our firm. My job was to protect him and to construct deals that provided the greatest opportunity for financial success within whatever creative endeavor he chose to explore. If my clients were successful, then I'd be successful. It didn't work the other way around. The truth is, that's the nature of enter-tainment law: it is built on the backs of the artists. Attorneys have notoriously big egos, and they (we) don't often like to admit it, but it's the client who makes the attorney.

We tried, vigorously but ultimately unsuccessfully, to expand our business beyond the music industry and into the world of athletics. It seemed to make sense: we were an African Ameri-can law firm, and a significant percentage of professional ath-letes in the most high-profile sports—basketball, football, and baseball—were persons of color. But it proved to be more chal-lenging than the entertainment business for a couple reasons: First, because Black agents and managers and attorneys had yet to make significant inroads in the sports realm; and sec-ond, because athletes were frequently targeted for representa-tion at an extremely young age. In basketball, for example, the top players often were introduced to agents while still playing

AAU ball in high school. By the time they got to college, they were all but locked up—if not officially, at least informally.

While I was still at Silverstein and Mullens, I got to know Patrick Ewing, who was then an NBA all-star with the New York Knicks. Patrick and my friend David were undergraduates together at Georgetown, and they remained close enough after graduation that Patrick would sometimes visit when he was in DC. During one of these visits, I took the opportunity to ask Patrick about the possibility of working with an African American agent or attorney. Patrick responded that indeed he would have considered Black representation had he been introduced to someone with the right credentials and personality when he was coming out of school. By this point, however, Patrick was deep into his career and satisfied with his current team of representatives.

A few years later, shortly after establishing our firm in New York, my partner and I met with the parents of Charlie Ward, a multitalented athlete who won the 1993 Heisman Trophy as a quarterback at Florida State, but who was expected to be a first-round pick in the upcoming NBA draft (he was the Seminoles' starting point guard, as well). Charlie's parents (and his sister) had graduated from Florida A&M, a public historically black university, and we had heard through the grapevine that they were committed to securing Black representation for their son. The meeting went well—pleasant and professional. In the end, though, they decided that we were simply too inexperienced in the field of sports law to be entrusted with Charlie's career.

There were other near misses, most notably Jamal Mashburn. Jamal had graduated from Cardinal Hayes High School in the Bronx before going on to lead Kentucky to a Final Four appearance in the 1993 NCAA tournament. He was the number four pick in the NBA draft and one of the most coveted players in the sport. As with many of our clients in the entertainment business, the path to the client in professional sports often went through Mom and Dad. We met with Jamal's mother and one of his cousins a few times, seemed to be making progress; we also heard that his father wanted Jamal to meet with us. But before we got a chance to sit down with him, he had signed with Bill Duffy, a white agent and attorney who had already begun to build an impressive roster of NBA clients.

We rather quickly abandoned pursuit of athletes in favor of strengthening our client base in the music field, but eventually we were able to meld the two interests by representing some athletes who ventured into the entertainment field. Among these, most notably, were Dale Davis and Wayman Tisdale, both of whom were first-round draft picks of the Indiana Pacers.

Dale remained on the management side of things by starting a record company and a production company. Wayman, meanwhile, rather famously left basketball while still quite capable of playing so that he could focus on his first love: playing jazz guitar and bass. It turned out that he was nearly as proficient a musician as he was an athlete—he recorded seven albums, including one that reached the top of *Billboard*'s contemporary jazz chart.

Meanwhile, our client list, still focused heavily on the music industry, continued to expand. We found new and promising artists, but we also became a destination firm for artists trying to make a commercial or creative shift. One of those was LL Cool J, one of the top performers in hip hop. He had recently hired a new manager named Charles Fisher, who was in the process of putting together an advisory and support team, including several new attorneys, to help LL not only deal with the cutthroat world of hip hop but also to capitalize on an expanding array of opportunities both in and out of the music industry. I had been introduced to Charles by Mike Abbott, the first African American VP at MCA Records.

I met LL at his grandmother's house in Queens. It was the same sort of discussion that I'd had with Pete Rock's family: "Trust me, and I'll help you get to the next level."

Truth is, while LL Cool J had already been to a pretty high level, he was still climbing, and there were changes that needed to be made, opportunities to be exploited, and contracts to be dissolved. In various stages of development were multiple endorsement deals (with, among others, Coca-Cola, Gap, and Major League Baseball), a television show with Quincy Jones, a book project with St. Martin's Press, a partnership with FUBU Apparel, and a record deal with Warner Music. Charles later explained to me that while LL's team already had a few lawyers on board, they wanted a trusted Black attorney's perspective on all contracts.

"When you have major surgery, you always get a second opinion, right?" Charles said.

"Right," I agreed.

"Well, you're our second opinion. On everything."

I felt like I was the right person for the job, and LL might have felt that way, too, but even a superstar from Queens needed his grandma's approval. That's just the way it worked in that world. I wasn't auditioning to become merely his attorney. I would be an adviser, a confidante, a family friend. Fortunately, LL's grandmother signed off on the arrangement, and we went to work. I helped him regain ownership of his master recordings, something that was almost unheard of in the hip hop world in those days (and is unusual even today). Recognizing LL's natural charm and talent, we began exploring even more opportunities outside music. He became one of the first hip hop artists to cross over into mainstream entertainment, building a diverse career in movies and television that endures to this day. Along the way, he received a second Grammy, and when he walked up onstage to receive the award, I felt proud to be part of his team.

My business partnership with Charles Fisher blossomed into a long-standing friendship based on our mutual interest in advocacy and social justice—in paying it forward. Charles founded a nonprofit called the Hip-Hop Summit Youth Council, for which I've done a lot of pro bono work. Over the last twenty years, the Hip-Hop Summit Youth Council has grown into one of the most significant social-service hip hop organizations in the world, thanks to partnerships with a broad range of supporters, including former president Barack Obama, former New York City mayor Bill de Blasio, the United Nations, Power 105.1/iHeart Media, and the New York City Police Department.

I'm grateful that my counsel has played some role in helping the organization grow and perhaps saved some youngsters from a life of crime and violence. I know all too well the risks of growing up in that environment.

In some ways, I've never left.

Chapter 11

YOU'VE GOT MY BACK,
I'VE GOT YOURS

For the first few years, at least, I spent a lot of time visiting artists in their natural habitat: the recording studio. Three or four times a week, I'd leave the office and the phones and the ledgers behind for a few hours and hang out with one of my clients while they did the work that was important to them. This was both a calculated display of loyalty—I was the rare attorney who spent any time in the recording studio, which demonstrated an investment beyond the merely financial—as well as a personal indulgence. I loved music and was fascinated by the creative process. Even then, in my thirties, I still sometimes daydreamed about what might have happened if I had chosen a different path when I was in high school, if I had thrown myself completely into the pursuit of a career in theater or film or television.

In some small way, watching up close while someone like Pete Rock turned a simple beat and a handful of words into a full-fledged epic filled that creative hole. Maybe I wasn't an artist myself, but at least I could support those who were, and I would have a front-row view to their development.

I got to work with some of the most talented people in the business, and in some cases I got to see them in the nascent stage of their careers. Among these was an aggressive and gifted young producer and rapper named Sean Combs.

Tony Dofat and Sean, better known at the time as Puff Daddy or Puffy, did a lot of work together in the early '90s, and since Tony was a client of mine, I was involved in shaping their contracts. Then, as now, Puffy was an intense guy, all business, no nonsense. A lot of musicians are not particularly fond of early mornings, but if there was business to attend to, Puffy would be on the phone as soon as the doors opened.

"Where's the contract?"

"Still working on it, Puffy."

"Well, work faster. Let's get it done."

I never doubted that Puffy would be a star, as well as a successful businessman. He was creative, driven, competitive. Not everyone liked him, which is pretty typical of someone who is hyperconfident. For a while, Puffy seemed to have his hand in a dozen projects at any given time, writing and recording his own material and producing records for others. This led to accusations, mostly born of jealousy, that Puffy was taking credit where perhaps none was due—that he would get a producer's or writer's credit when actually he hadn't spent that much time in the studio. But I had seen his work ethic, and I knew of his reputation among the artists with whom he worked. Puffy's gift was taking something good and transforming it into something great.

For the better part of a decade, our firm thrived, with a client list that included our first big clients Pete Rock & CL Smooth, but also Busta Rhymes, MC Lyte, SWV, Changing Faces, Lost Boyz, Jazzy Jeff, Big L, Heavy D, Junior M.A.F.I.A., and Lil' Kim. With the last two came office visits from their mentor, the Notorious B.I.G. (Biggie Smalls), and with Biggie came disquieting proximity to the heat of the East Coast–West Coast rap wars.

This was, to put it mildly, a tumultuous period in the music industry, with so many performers having risen from the streets and still connected, either tangentially or explicitly, to the gangs and the drugs and violence that swirled around them. In some ways, I was no different. I'd just had the good fortune to get out.

But there were days when I felt that I hadn't quite escaped entirely, like the time a business acquaintance showed up at my office, with some of his entourage, and spread out a half dozen firearms on my desk.

I'd known this guy for a while, at least since my return to New York. He had long been attached to various illicit moneymaking activities and questionable associates. Now, like a lot of ambitious young Black men, he was in the process of trying to penetrate the world of hip hop and rap. He had developed a small production company and attracted a handful of artists, some of whom were not without talent. But the business was brutally competitive, and while I helped him try to further the careers of some of these artists, none broke through in a major way.

For a period of time, though, I was drawn into his network. He was a client, and his idea of reciprocation for my services involved not just a legal fee, but practical, real-world protection. And here it was, right now, resting on my desk.

"Go ahead," he said, waving a hand proudly over the arsenal. "Take your pick."

I leaned back in my chair, held up my hands, making sure I didn't touch anything. I had no idea whose bodies were all over those guns.

"No, thanks."

"Hey, nothing wrong with being able to defend yourself," he said. "In case you haven't noticed, shit is real out there."

I nodded in recognition. People in and around the music industry were getting shot and killed, arrested and put away. And I had no intention of joining their ranks in any capacity whatsoever.

"Appreciate the gesture, but I'm good."

"Suit yourself, man."

This was a unique, exciting time in the music industry. Not since the heyday of Motown had there been so many opportunities for talented, ambitious Black artists to break into the mainstream. Rap and hip hop, arrogantly dismissed in the early '80s as a novelty by white audiences and executives alike, had taken root in the popular culture and was rapidly crossing racial and socioeconomic divides. By the mid-1990s, it had become the dominant genre in commercial music, elbowing out grunge and pop and metal—and even classic rock—for space on the airwaves and in clubs and other venues.

Especially appealing, from the artists' perspective, was that there was a decidedly homegrown approach to rap and hip hop that gave performers, DJs, and producers more control over their material and careers than perhaps they had ever known. And while the presentation and lyrics—thick with stories of violence and crime and drugs and sex—terrified much of white America, they resonated with young Black audiences. And, increasingly, with young white listeners as well. The truth is, if you wanted a corollary for rap or hip hop, you needn't have looked any further than the roots of country music, a predominantly white genre whose practitioners wrote and sang of the common man, in lyrics that, while not as explicit, certainly trafficked in themes familiar to rap audiences: specifically, fighting and fucking.

Today, of course, mash-ups are the rule, rather than the exception, with lines between genres so blurred as to be almost unrecognizable. And you will be hard-pressed to find a current artist, in any genre, who wasn't influenced by rap and hip hop. Moreover, the SoundCloud revolution, which spawned a generation of self-made artists in all genres unencumbered by the studio system or the limits of antiquated technology, is simply a natural outgrowth of the DIY mentality so prevalent in early hip hop.

If there was a significant drawback to the rise of rap and hip hop, it was the extent to which life imitated art. In many cases, the artists and producers and DJs who dominated the scene in the 1990s rose from the very streets and circumstances so forcefully and vividly depicted in their music. Some had been involved in gangs; others were still actively involved, or at the very least welcomed a criminal presence in their entourages. This was more common in West Coast circles than East Coast, but certainly there were examples from both camps of careers being buoyed by money that was, for lack of a better term, dirty. Unquestionably, there was a period of time during which association with certain artists carried a degree of legitimate danger—the murders of Tupac Shakur and Biggie Smalls being the most glaring examples.

Thus the weaponry spread out across my office desk, offered not as a flamboyant display of muscle but as a gesture of goodwill.

You've got my back, I've got yours.

But here's where things got tricky. As audiences increasingly embraced not just the music but also the violence and danger so often depicted, there arose a weirdly romantic notion about what it meant to be a rapper or hip hop artist, along with expectations that the artists themselves had lived these experiences and were not mere poseurs. For artists who lacked "street cred," and for those of us who worked with artists of all types, this was a challenging phenomenon. In some ways, it actually became an advantage—a cynical marketing tool—for an artist to have spent time in jail or prison, or to be able to legitimately claim association with gangs such as the Crips or the Bloods.

This was a wild period in the music industry, unlike anything seen before or since, with outright criminals frequently involved in the shaping of careers, and artists themselves sometimes feigning criminal personas to boost their credibility and increase sales. We all knew that, from a marketing standpoint, controversy could help an artist. The audience wanted to believe that you weren't just making shit up (as artists have done for centuries), but that you could prove that you had actually lived the experiences in your songs. Unfortunately, this sort of behavior, real or implied, could also get you killed.

As an attorney, I had no desire to spend much time doing damage control. I wanted my clients to avoid trouble and focus on their music and their careers. I also disliked the idea of promoting or condoning violence, but this was a tightrope you walked every day in the hip hop world. Some things were beyond your control.

Given our youthful clientele, the job very quickly developed into much more than simply vetting and negotiating contracts. Our firm tried to teach financial literacy, still woefully lacking among talent across the entire spectrum of the entertainment industry (including among professional athletes). Most of these artists had come from little. When suddenly flush with money, they had no idea how to respond. There were family members to support, friends with their hands out. There was an overwhelming urge to flaunt their newfound success. The result, as often as not, was an orgy of spending that could leave the artist virtually broke in a matter of months.

"Pretend it's not even there," I'd suggest. "At least for a little while. Put it in the bank. Focus on your work."

Sometimes they'd listen. Sometimes not. It was painful to watch real wealth slip through their fingers like Monopoly money, when even a modicum of restraint could have set them up for life. I understood how they felt. I had been poor. I knew what it was like to want things I couldn't afford. But I had accrued resources slowly, over a number of years. I had studied and trained; I had multiple degrees; I had been mentored.

A twentysomething-year-old rapper who had never had more than a few hundred bucks in his checking account (if he even had a checking account) and now suddenly had a six-figure recording or production deal? That kid was unlikely to be fiscally prudent.

One of my clients was a young man named Alex Richbourg, who was briefly part of Trackmasters, one of the most successful production teams of the '90s (the lineup of artists who worked with Trackmasters includes Jay-Z, 50 Cent, Mary J. Blige, the Notorious B.I.G., Jennifer Lopez, and Mariah Carey).

At one point, Trackmasters Entertainment (a corporate entity that was also one of our clients) received a substantial payment. Alex's cut, at the time, was the largest payday of his career by a wide margin—and he immediately decided to go out and buy a new car.

"Be careful," I said. "Think about what you need instead of what you want."

Alex looked at me as though I were speaking a different language. "What are you talkin' about?"

"Don't spend your money. That's what people do in this industry—they spend the money as soon as it comes in the door. That's not what rich people do; it's what poor people do."

"Yeah?"

"Sometimes you can't even tell when someone's rich," I continued. "They don't flash a bunch of jewelry or go on big vacations. But if you visit them at home, you might notice they have a really nice place. They don't show off. They don't care what other people think. They're *quietly* wealthy."

Alex nodded in approval to show me he was getting it.

"You know what else?" I added. "They *stay* wealthy."

A few days later, I drove Alex to a Toyota dealership in New Jersey, where he picked out a perfectly pleasant Toyota Camry. A functional set of wheels. Cost about eighteen thousand dollars.

"Good job," I said, proudly shaking his hand. "Enjoy the ride."

Alex nodded and drove off with a smile on his face, looking very much like a quietly wealthy young man.

Two weeks later, I heard from a mutual acquaintance that Alex had returned the Camry and picked up a new BMW. Next time I saw him, I just shook my head.

"Alex . . . what did you do?"

He shrugged, laughed.

"It's the pressure, man. I can't be seen driving a Camry. I'm sorry."

The most disappointing part of that story is that Alex was smart enough to know what he should have done. But the music industry was such a flashy, self-indulgent world. Encouraging fiscal responsibility, I realized, wasn't enough. These young people needed education and support, and this opened the door of opportunity for African American professionals who otherwise might not have had a chance to work with high-profile recording artists and producers. While men and women of color were increasingly prevalent on the creative end of things, the business was still dominated by the same demographic that had always run the entertainment industry: white males (typically beyond middle age). Our firm had begun to break through some of those barriers, and I felt like part of our mission was to facilitate opportunities for other Black men and women who were every bit as capable as their white counterparts; they simply needed a chance to prove it.

One of the legendary behind-the-scenes figures in the entertainment business was a man named Bert Padell, a New York–based accountant, financial adviser, and tax attorney whose career spanned nearly six decades. Bert grew up in the Bronx and became a batboy for his beloved Yankees in the late 1940s, when he was in his teens, a period in which he befriended and collected signed memorabilia from the likes of Whitey Ford, Yogi Berra, and Joe DiMaggio (who later became a client). In addition to many sports stars of the 1960s and '70s, Bert amassed a client list that included some of the biggest names in Hollywood, such as Robert De Niro and Faye Dunaway.

But it was in the music business that Bert became most well-known, thanks to an astonishingly deep and eclectic roster of artists representing a wide array of genres, from Britney Spears to Blondie; from the Talking Heads to Alicia Keys; from Pink Floyd to the Notorious B.I.G., who immortalized Bert in 112's song "Only You."

> Room 112, *where the players dwell*
> *And stash more cash than Bert Padell*

Far from being an indictment of Bert's character, this was Biggie's stamp of approval—name-checking the man who had advised him and countless other artists on the mundane but critically important topics of money management and accounting. In the early days of rap and hip hop, Bert was frequently a front line of defense for young Black artists suddenly thrust into the public eye and earning more money than they ever imagined possible. These included such pioneers as Rakim, Run-DMC, Kurtis Blow, and Puff Daddy.

You would be hard-pressed to find anyone who has an unkind word for Bert. His passing in 2018 prompted a flood of tributes and heartfelt sentiment from those whose careers he helped guide and whose security he valued. He was a sweet man who self-published several books of poetry and began most correspondence with the words, "Hey, babe." So, you'll find no criticism of the man or his abilities here. Bert was a consummate professional who earned his success and believed strongly in the power of philanthropy. In short, like me, Bert was a proponent of both fiscal conservatism and paying it forward, a philosophy he encouraged to his clients once they achieved a level of financial security.

Despite these professional and philosophical similarities, Bert and I had a somewhat rocky relationship. I would not automatically steer my clients to his practice, as so many other entertainment attorneys did. This naturally disappointed Bert, as he had a solid track record, and my firm represented a growing roster of musicians.

"What's the problem?" Bert would say. "Have I done something to offend you?"

"Not at all, Bert. I'm just presenting my clients with choices."

It wasn't personal, I explained. I simply wanted to involve people who did not ordinarily have an opportunity to represent the top artists. I was trying to help level the playing field.

Some of my clients ended up hiring Bert, which was fine. Some did not and chose instead to work with Vernon Brown, an African American accountant whose work I knew to be very strong. But Bert did not surrender quietly. If one of my clients chose a different accountant, he would inquire as to their financial investment strategy. These were separate cogs in the financial machinery, and Bert prided himself on being multitalented.

Not intending to disrespect Bert or his work, I continued to push for talented professionals whose ethnic background (and/or gender) had historically precluded a seat at the grown-ups' table. Opponents of diversity initiatives will frequently argue that all hires should be based exclusively on the strength of a résumé; that a sheet of paper should dictate who gets the job. Simple as that. But that is a painfully naive and antiquated notion that reflects either ignorance or willful disregard for the way the world actually works, and the history of systemic racism in the United States, across virtually all institutions.

Simply put, race matters, because race is often an impediment to educational, professional, and socioeconomic advancement. For so many Black kids, merely getting to the starting line (in the form of a stable home environment, strong secondary education, or college degree) is a daunting challenge. Similarly, for a talented Black professional, it often isn't so much a case of whether he or she is capable of doing the job; it's whether they're even aware that the job exists.

I would never have steered one of my clients to an adviser simply because the adviser was a person of color, but I would absolutely present an exceptional person of color who might lack the on-paper credentials of someone from a more privileged background as a fully viable candidate for the job. Because they were.

To that end, I recruited Robert Henderson and Ameena Ali from the Henderson Financial Group, a pair of African American financial advisers from Florida, to work with some of our clients. They were both sharp and personable, with an impressive portfolio. I'd known Ameena for a while but had never met Robert (her partner) prior to their first trip to New York. It was clear from the outset that he was highly astute and at least Ameena's equal when it came to financial matters. Where he was not Ameena's equal was in the realm of fashion. Robert was a country boy, and he dressed the part: jeans, boots, open-collar shirts.

"No offense," I said toward the end of the meeting. "But we're going to have to go shopping."

Ameena smiled, lowered her head. I laughed.

"Sorry, but that cowboy act won't fly up here."

We spent the afternoon driving around Manhattan, guiding Robert on an epic shopping excursion. The longer it went on, the more his ego recovered.

"I kind of like this," he said, checking himself out in a Bloomingdale's mirror.

"You should," Ameena said. "You look good."

(As an aside—not long before that day, I had been compelled to follow my own advice about conveying a certain image. On a trip to meet an up-and-coming young R&B group named Soul for Real, our firm rented a Cadillac because, frankly, the Dodge Dart no longer exuded the level of success we or our clients aspired to. By the time I met Robert, I had upgraded to a BMW.)

The day was not entirely smooth. In the afternoon, approaching rush hour, we were cruising north on Eighth

Avenue, between Fifty-Sixth and Fifty-Seventh Street, when I spotted a Black man on the curb, trying to flag down a taxi. Pedestrians hailing cabs is an all-day occurrence in Manhattan, so I'm not sure why this one caught my eye for more than a split second. But it did. And what I saw was this: a cab, also driving north, apparently spotting the Black man and pulling over to the curb . . . except not stopping. Instead, it crept along the parking lane, a few feet at a time, until it came to a stop in front of a different customer: a white couple, well-dressed, holding umbrellas to fend off the rain.

I saw the couple open the door and start to get in. And I saw the Black man, maybe ten or fifteen feet down the road, shake his head and raise his hand, trying to hail a different taxi.

"That's some bullshit, right there," I said, feeling the blood rush to my head.

"What happened?" Robert asked. He hadn't even noticed.

"That taxi . . . ," I said, the words drifting off. And then I yanked the steering wheel to the right, oblivious to the consequences, and guided my car from the center lane to the curb. As horns blasted all around us, I pulled in front of the taxi and parked at a 45-degree angle, effectively boxing him in.

"Uh, what are you doing?" Ameena asked.

"Just going to talk to this guy."

"You sure that's a good idea?"

"Uh-huh."

Truth is, I wasn't sure. I wasn't even thinking straight. I just knew what I had seen: a taxi driving right past a Black customer in favor of a white customer. Why the driver did this, I couldn't say. And I didn't care. I reacted with the same sort of primal rage that had nearly gotten me in trouble in the past. That there was a lot more at stake now didn't seem to matter.

Right was right.

This was wrong.

"Hey, buddy," I said, rapping on the cabdriver's window. "Open up."

The driver rolled down the window. He was a white guy, maybe in his fifties, but he was sort of beat down, so it was hard to tell.

"What's the problem?" he said, his voice indicating he knew exactly what the problem was.

I took a deep breath, looked at the white couple now seated comfortably in the back. And then I looked back at the Black man, a young guy, maybe in his late twenties or early thirties, casually but neatly dressed, standing in the rain, and I couldn't help but think, *That guy could be me; hell, he was me.*

"Why did you pass the brother?" I asked.

The cabbie glanced furtively out the window.

"I didn't see him."

"You couldn't have not seen him. You drove right by him."

The driver shrugged, said nothing. I looked into the back seat; the white couple seemed to be getting nervous.

"You two," I said. "Out. Now."

"Why?" the man asked.

"Because that gentleman"—I gestured to the Black man at the curb—"was waiting in line ahead of you. This is his ride."

The white couple exited the cab and walked away as I held the back door open.

"All yours," I said, as the Black man entered the cab.

"Thanks."

I shut the door and leaned into the cabbie's window. "Now take this man where he needs to go."

I got back into the car, my heart racing, and sat there for a moment, trying to calm down. Ameena and Robert were silent. As we started to pull away, Ameena said, "Damn, Bruce! That was like Superman."

I shook my head. "Nah, I'm just sick of this shit."

We hadn't gone more than two blocks when an NYPD patrol car came up behind us, lights flashing, sirens blaring. I pulled to the curb again.

Well, that didn't take long.

"What's going on?" Robert asked.

"We'll see. Don't say anything."

I rolled down the window and sat perfectly still, both hands on the wheel. A white cop approached the vehicle, skipped right over the "license and registration" protocol, and cut to the chase.

"I saw you pull in front of that taxi back there," he said. "What was that all about?"

"You *saw* it?" I repeated.

"Yeah."

"Like, you witnessed the incident . . . or someone reported it to you?"

The officer took a deep breath.

"You can't cut in front of a taxi. And you can't start a fight in the street."

"That's not what happened, Officer," I said, trying to remain calm. And then I proceeded to explain what had transpired, how the cab had ignored a Black customer in favor of a white customer. "I just wanted to make sure the young man got his rightful opportunity to ride in that cab," I continued. "Is that a crime?"

In fact, it may have been a crime. At the very least, using your car to intercept a taxi in the middle of a Manhattan rush hour likely violates some sort of traffic ordinance. But I didn't care. I was on the side of right, and we both knew it.

"Just don't do it again," the cop said. "And drive carefully."

"Yes, sir. Thank you, Officer."

As we pulled away and began driving back to my office, Robert laughed. "Is it always like this in New York?"

"Too often," I said.

I'd like to say that a desire to further the causes of social justice and equity—of diversity and inclusion—fueled my tendency to seek out African American colleagues in finance and investment and management. And that would be true—to a point. But it wouldn't be the entire truth. Some of it—maybe a lot of it—was personal, residue from a childhood shaped by poverty, and racism that presented itself on a regular basis, whether in the form of a taxi driver bypassing a Black passenger in favor of a white one, a cop profiling a Black man on the street, or music-industry executives surreptitiously (or sometimes overtly) trying to convince Black artists that their careers were better off in the hands of white managers, attorneys, accountants, and agents.

I took this personally, and I did not take it lying down.

By the mid 1990s, Trackmasters Entertainment had developed into one of the most influential production entities in rap and hip hop. It had also acquired a new manager named Steve

Stoute, who, among other things, changed the band's name from its original spelling (TrackMasterz) to the more commonly recognized Trackmasters. Stoute would go on to have a prominent career in music, including stints as president of the Urban Music division of Interscope Geffen A&M Records, and president of Urban Music for Sony Music Entertainment. Prior to that, he managed the careers of Mary J. Blige and Nas, as well as Trackmasters.

It was while managing Trackmasters that Stoute, an African American, encouraged his clients to sever their ties with my firm and begin working with Joel Katz, a highly regarded and powerful media attorney from Atlanta who had gotten his big break in the business many years earlier, when he began representing James Brown. It was Stoute's contention that Katz was more capable of negotiating with record labels on behalf of Trackmasters; that, in fact, as a white attorney in a predominantly white industry, he would be able to secure for Trackmasters a better contract than our firm could negotiate.

That this argument was put forth by a Black man—an industry insider, no less—only made it more galling. I raise this point not to single out Steve, but to address the larger point of Black professionals, particularly in the entertainment industry, facing hurdles not faced by others in building a client roster and selling our services. (While progress has been made, this remains true even today.) I wanted to do my part by promoting diversity in the area of professional services without ever compromising competency and skillset.

In the end, I negotiated a deal with Elektra Records on behalf of Trackmasters. Steve Stoute then took the deal memo

I had put together and presented it to Sony, which matched the Elektra offer. Trackmasters ultimately accepted the Sony offer, with Joel Katz as the attorney of record. Life is not always fair, but I felt like the point had been made. The best attorney negotiates the best contract, regardless of race.

I began my career with a spirit of aggression and survivalism that fit the way I was raised, in an environment that rewarded toughness and brutalized the weak. Too, there was an element of retribution—a desire to extract a pound of flesh from the unscrupulous white industry executives who for years (decades) had taken advantage of Black artists. I became known as one of the toughest negotiators in the rap genre, a reputation I frankly took as a compliment, but which also grew to become counterproductive.

After a conversation with Elektra Records president Sylvia Rhone, a frequent and respected business partner, my colleague Denise Brown sat me down and delivered some harsh news.

"Bruce, you've got to lighten up a little," she said. "A lot of these executives are starting to resent you."

My reply was typical of that time in my life: "Your point is?"

Denise laughed. "My point is this: It's all about presentation, how you do it. You can still get what you want, but in the end, both parties have to feel good about the process."

That conversation stayed with me. It put a dent in my ego and forced me to confront the fact that I was getting cocky and putting myself and my clients at risk. Confidence is one thing; arrogance is quite another, and it can blind you to the truth of your circumstances and how others view your behavior.

I saw this occasionally from the other side, as well, like when Andre Harrell became CEO of Motown Records in the mid-'90s. Andre was a brilliant young producer and executive, having worked with Russell Simmons at Def Jam before founding Uptown Records while still in his twenties. There he signed such artists as Guy, Heavy D, Mary J. Blige, and Jodeci; he also brought in Puff Daddy as an A&R executive. With the soaring popularity of rap and hip hop, Andre became one of the most influential executives in music, a stature that prompted his recruitment to Motown, which was trying to recapture the prominence of its heyday.

In his new position, Andre oversaw a campaign called "Uptown to Motown," which was intended to reflect the venerable label's resurgence—bringing the flavor of Uptown to Motown. But the perception was something else entirely. From the outside, it seemed that Andre was making it all about himself rather than the artists he was recruiting or the music they produced. Andre created a lot of Black millionaires, and at the end of the day he was all about empowering Black people and presenting opportunities to Black artists. He was trying to use his brand to create an atmosphere in which young artists would feel comfortable coming back to Motown, which they viewed as their parents' (or grandparents') record label. But the message was getting lost, and it was pissing off corporate America. And Andre didn't even realize it.

I knew this because I represented several artists who were signed to either Uptown or Motown. I heard the gossip, the blowback, about how record-label executives were supposed to stay in the background and take care of business. They were not supposed to hog the spotlight. And I decided to share some of it with Andre, because I wanted him to stay in power. I wanted to see a young Black man succeed at the highest echelon of our business.

"Andre, you have to tone down the act a little," I suggested. "Focus on making more money for your corporation. That's all that matters."

Andre seemed almost amused.

"That's what I'm trying to do."

"I know, but sometimes it's about optics," I said. "And this doesn't look good."

We all grow and, hopefully, evolve. Andre continued to be a dominant force in music. I learned to drive a hard bargain with a smile. I learned to be satisfied with a victory that did not include a public evisceration of my opponent. I became a better attorney.

Not that the industry was any less volatile.

In the late 1990s, we began representing a hip hop group called the Lost Boyz, four kids from Queens who had already enjoyed a run of gold records and critical acclaim but had been in a bit of a lull the previous two years. Our job was to help them regain some of that success, but with more substantial financial rewards and a firmer hand on their own careers. On the night of March 28, 1999, one of the group's members, a young man named Tahliq Raymond Rogers (AKA Freaky Tah), was shot and killed while leaving a birthday party for another group member at the Sheraton Hotel in Queens. As it turned out, Freaky Tah was simply in the wrong place at the wrong time, a bystander caught in the crossfire of someone else's conflict.

I spent the next several days on the business of death, working with Tah's accountant to find life insurance documents, making sure that the roughly $70,000 check he had picked up from our office on the day he was killed made it into his bank account, and helping his family access those funds. Tah was twenty-seven years old, and his death hit me hard, reminding me again of all the young Black men I had known who had died too early or were wasting away behind bars.

Unfortunately, Tah was not the only client we lost to senseless violence. That same year, a burgeoning rap superstar named Lamont "Big L" Coleman—a client who in a very short time had put himself on track to legendary status within his industry—was gunned down in a drive-by shooting not far from where he had grown up. He was twenty-four years old. So much violence . . . so much promise unfulfilled. And indelible reminders of the value of my work to my clients, their families, and the communities they came from.

Chapter 12

FIRST AND FOREMOST

South Bronx, New York, 1995

With a clipboard in hand, in some of the most danger-ous neighborhoods in New York, I wandered from house to house, apartment to apartment, knocking on doors, intro-ducing myself, explaining my platform, asking for signatures. At least that's what I did in the rare instances someone both-ered to answer the door.

A couple years earlier, I had moved to the Soundview sec-tion of the Bronx, where my girlfriend, Tania, had a home. By this time, we had a growing family and dual careers, lives on an ever-quickening treadmill. For me, that wasn't enough. There were deals to be made, careers to advance, causes to champion. I logged seventy, eighty hours per week at the office, convinced that the tireless work ethic that had gotten me through Georgetown and into the upper echelon of enter-tainment law would sustain other ventures as well.

I wanted to be a facilitator of change, of progress. I wanted to be of service, both within the legal and entertainment fields, and in my personal life. And I didn't want to be seen as a wealthy brother who forgot his roots. That meant making commitments to diversity and inclusion—encouraging opportunities for Black attorneys, accountants, financial advisers, and artists—and it also meant rolling up my sleeves and getting involved in community affairs and politics at a local level.

Trust me, it doesn't get any more local, or personal, than running for the school board.

My district was roughly 90 percent Black and Latino. The remaining 10 percent was Caucasian, mostly Italian Americans from the neighboring Throgs Neck neighborhood. Despite this, people of color were barely represented on the school board—typically filling just one of seven available seats. The reason? Turnout among Black and Latino voters was historically low, bordering on abysmal. White voters, on the other hand, turned out in droves and made sure their kids—and their kids' schools' prerogatives—were served first and foremost. In New York City, local school boards wielded tremendous power and discretion over financial resources. Without an increase in Black and Latino representation at the local level, the rich would continue to get richer, and the poor would continue to get poorer.

The fix seemed simple: Canvass the neighborhoods. Get out the vote. Educate people on the importance of community involvement, and especially of improving the quality of schools.

Rather than being content to support another candidate, I threw my hat in the ring and ran for a position on the school board. The campaign exposed both my political inexperience and my naivete.

Or maybe it was arrogance. I had grown up in the projects. I had attended substandard schools. I had been a first-
hand witness to crime and violence and racism. I presumed,
therefore, that these experiences had made me somewhat
bulletproof, that the good folks of the South Bronx would
open their doors, offer welcoming hugs, patiently listen to
monologues and stump speeches about the importance of
education and representation.

"This is your neighborhood, your school district," I
would tell them. "Own it!"

Then I would hand them my clipboard and ask for their
support, and they would eagerly oblige. I'd have the required
number of signatures to get on the ballot in no time. And then
I'd win the election and become a true agent of socioeconomic
change, at the grass-roots level, where it matters most.

Except it didn't quite work out that way.

The collecting of signatures would take me into some
of the city's roughest neighborhoods and housing projects,
an experience I felt I could handle. But while discussing
my potential candidacy one day with a client who had inti-
mate familiarity with the South Bronx, I was given a reality check.

"You can't just walk in there like you own the place," he
said. "No one knows who you are. It's not safe."

"Come on, man. I live in the Bronx."

"You live in Soundview."

"Yeah?"

He smiled, shrugged. I got the point. Soundview was not
exactly Tribeca—in fact, it might have been worse than most
of the South Bronx neighborhoods in which I planned to

canvass. But that wasn't the point. The point was, once I left Soundview, I was an outsider.

"Listen," he said. "I'll go with you. Most people over there know me. You'll be okay."

Truthfully, I wasn't sure whether he would protect me or attract an element that might make the endeavor more dangerous. See, this was the same guy who had placed an assortment of firearms on my desk and encouraged me to take my pick. This was not a man prone to deescalating volatile situations. Then again, painful as it might be to admit, there are times when a little muscle, or at least a familiar face, comes in handy. This was one of those occasions.

He suggested we visit the Forest Houses, a massive housing project in the Morrisania section of the Bronx. With some thirteen hundred apartments in fifteen buildings, all stretching between nine and fourteen stories in height, the Forest Houses were home to more than three thousand New Yorkers, most on public assistance. It was not dissimilar to the Amsterdam Houses, in that it was basically a small, self-contained, self-regulated city, with an assortment of problems related to crime and drugs and poverty. But the South Bronx was a more dangerous place than Upper Manhattan, and the Forest Houses was by degrees a more dangerous place than the Amsterdam Houses. Especially if you were considered an interloper.

"Here's what we're going to do," my friend suggested. "We'll go over there, we'll stand outside together, and as people come out, you can introduce yourself, and we'll get all the signatures you need. It'll be fine. Lot easier than going door-to-door."

"Okay, whatever you say."

So, that's what we did. And for a while it went well. Some people were willing to talk and sign, some people were not, but over the course of a few hours I had amassed a few dozen signatures. It was tedious, time-consuming work; it was also, I believed, part of the foundation on which a democratic society was built. I can't say I enjoyed it, but I knew it was important. After a while, though, my friend grew restless.

"I'm going to run to the store," he said. "Stay right in this neighborhood. Don't go wandering off."

I did not wander off. I continued to collect signatures for the next hour, until my friend finally returned. There was an urgency to his gait as he approached.

"We need to get out of here."

"Why? What's up?"

"Maybe nothing. Maybe trouble. Better to not find out."

Apparently, my presence in the neighborhood had attracted undue attention, especially in the brief period when I was alone. Someone had spoken up, made a scene of it, and pegged me as an undercover cop nosing about in the area.

Nah, that's my boy, my friend had corrected him. *He's running for school board. Just getting signatures, that's all.*

School board? the acquaintance had said. *Shit . . .*

Yeah, call it off, my friend directed.

Not sure I can do that, the acquaintance explained. *Word is out.*

"Man, I'm glad you're with me," I said.

My friend nodded. "Let's go."

I'd eventually accumulate enough signatures to get on the ballot, but the real race proved even harder. I fell short on election day, and the board remained overwhelmingly Caucasian, continuing the underrepresentation of the predominantly Black and Latino schools of the area. This was a devastating lesson in local politics, as well as the politics of race, of which I incorrectly presumed myself an astute observer. It turns out, I didn't know what I didn't know.

As expected, I had lost the white vote. Badly. But what I discovered afterward is that I had lost the Latino vote as well. It turned out that the three largest demographics in the district—white, Black, and Latino—were, predictably, most likely to vote first for a candidate who matched their own ethnicity. But things got tricky after that: Black voters tended to vote first for a Black candidate, second for a Latino candidate, and third for a white candidate. Latino voters, however, voted Latino first, white second, Black third. In so doing, we were almost guaranteed a school board comprising white candidates who would apportion funds to the schools that needed them least: those serving a predominantly white and affluent (or at least middle-class) population. In a very real sense, the voters were working against their own self-interests.

This was somehow the worst result of it all. It was hard enough to overcome traditionally low turnout among Black and Latino voters, but to see the details of how the voting shook out was confounding . . . and depressing. I was among the most qualified candidates on the ballot: a Georgetown-educated attorney with an advanced degree, a thriving practice in entertainment law, a client list primarily of artists of color (many from New York), and two small children who would one day be students in the district.

But at the end of the day, I was still a Black man, and that alone sewed enough suspicion and mistrust to sink my candidacy.

A body in motion tends to stay in motion; a body at rest tends to stay at rest. Physics, of course, but I found it applicable to everyday life. And so, with Longfellow's words continually echoing in my head, I kept climbing St. Augustine's ladder, secure in the knowledge that I could reach the heights of great men—so long as I eschewed sleep and other distractions, and stayed focused on the things that mattered, and kept pushing and reaching, relentlessly striving, day after unrelenting day.

There was a cost. My relationship with Tania was complicated by a number of issues, not least the fact that she was my first love, and those are hard to get over. We broke up, got together, broke up again, got together again . . . etc. That our relationship had somehow survived the dubious claim of paternity while I was in law school was something of a miracle, and one I can't explain except to say that love is unreasonable, irrational, glorious, painful, and heartbreaking—sometimes all in the same day. And marriage—or a long-term partnership, such as ours—requires much more than a casual commitment. You start out with the best of intentions, and you wake up a few years later to discover that whatever you had was gone. Maybe it's your fault; maybe it's your partner's fault. Most likely, each party bears some responsibility. And if they don't, you try to move forward.

By the time Tania and I moved in together, her daughter, Jenell, was six years old. Within a year, our daughter Sabree was born. A year after that, we had another daughter named Maya. We moved out of the Bronx and bought a house in Mount Vernon, a comparatively leafy suburb on the southern tip of Westchester County.

In what felt like the blink of an eye, my life had been completely transformed. We weren't married, but I considered myself to be a partner, and while Jenell was not my biological daughter, I considered myself her father. I was responsible for a family of five now (in addition to helping support my mother and, eventually, my father). There was no time in the day, nor any place in my psyche, to analyze what it meant to be a father or a partner, or to evaluate whether I was meeting the multiple demands of the role. I knew what it meant—or thought I did—because I had grown up without a father. My family had been poor, but what I resented most was the mere fact of his absence, the complete abdication of responsibility. Did I miss the affection of a father? The guidance? Walking together in the park, my little hand lost in his? Maybe so, but as an adult, I didn't give it much thought. I knew only that, right then, with a full house in Mount Vernon, my job was to put food on the table and make sure my kids had a safe and stable living environment.

Whether I was around to give them baths or help with homework or even to share family dinners was, to me, irrelevant. I was, first and foremost, a provider. Not that Tania didn't work, as well. She had transferred from Hofstra, obtained a degree from Lehman College, and worked as a bookkeeper. But I was the primary breadwinner by a wide margin, and I took pride in that distinction, for it drew a clear line between me and my father, and between me and many other men I had known when I was a kid. My children would never have to wonder whether the rent would be paid. They would not have to accept public assistance. They could count on their dad. No matter what, I would never abandon them.

So, I threw myself into my work. Accumulating resources for our security came first (and probably second and third, as well). It was easy enough to rationalize the imbalance.

Things got complicated after a few years, when Tania and I drifted apart; our relationship floundered, became contentious, and she decided to leave. She moved into an apartment with her cousin in the Bronx, while I stayed in the house in Mount Vernon, with all three children. They visited their mother on the weekends, but for all practical purposes, I was thrust into the role of single father. I did so with help, yes—paid and volunteer. Family members chipped in. I had a new girlfriend (but not a new friend, as we had known each other since the Hofstra days) named Denyce who helped take care of the girls as if they were her own. And I did my best to balance work and family. I told bedtime stories, read books, tried to get home in time for dinner, and even did the cooking myself some days.

No, I was not Mr. Mom, but neither was I a distant, emotionally negligent father. I was a dad, imperfect but present, careening through a turbulent period in my life and doing the best I could. Work was my anchor, the office and recording studios sanctuaries where I felt confident, alive. Whatever shortcomings I may have had around the house, I sought to offset them at my job. There, at least, I had some semblance of control.

There was a custody battle, intense and prolonged. It was my contention that the girls were better off in my home, in part because of my ability to provide for them financially, but also because this was where they had spent the majority of their time, both before and after the separation. This was their home. I sought primary custody, knowing it would be an uphill battle. Family courts even today do not generally favor the father in a custody dispute, and they certainly didn't favor the father in the 1990s. As part of the court's due diligence, I was required to undergo a psychological evaluation to determine my parental "fitness." In the end, while the court had no quarrel with my financial capabilities, nor any issues with whether the girls would be in a healthy home environment—one in which education would obviously be of paramount importance—it nevertheless decided that the girls would be better served in Tania's sole custody.

"We have no doubt you're a good father," the judge began, by way of explanation. "But the psychological evaluation indicates that you are not really in touch with your feelings, and that could be a detriment to the children."

I took a deep breath, tried to suppress the simmering rage that now threatened to erupt and provide an ugly demonstration of just how in touch with my feelings I really was.

"Your Honor, with all due respect," I began, addressing the white male judge, advised by the white male psychologist, and the white female law guardian representing my children, "I don't think you understand Black culture. Most Black men are not warm and fuzzy. That's not the way we are raised.

You're making assumptions about Black kids and Black families and Black fathers, and if you're wrong on this one, you won't be there for the fallout. I'll be there."

I paused.

"To be perfectly candid, I feel like I'm being bamboozled here."

Bamboozled. It's generally unwise to walk into a custody hearing, or any hearing, for that matter, and insult the judge who holds your fate in his hands, but by this point I knew what had been lost. Here I had been the primary custodial parent of three children—including one who was not my own—for the better part of a year. I had demonstrated both the ability and the desire to provide them with the best possible home environment. I was actively involved at school, where the teachers all knew me by name. But because they were girls, and I was a man—a Black man apparently untethered from his *feelings*—it was presumed that they would be better served by living primarily with their mother. I would retain only visitation rights.

When the hearing ended, I went home and shared the news with the girls. Though it broke my heart, I helped them pack their suitcases and told them everything would be okay. On the way to their mom's place, we stopped at McDonald's for ice cream. More laughter, more promises of a happy life. I dropped them off, kissed them goodbye, told them I would see them in a few days, and drove away.

I waited until I was out of sight to cry.

One measure of a man is how well he copes with adversity . . . with disappointment. I'd known my share and had always considered myself more resilient than most people, but the custody dispute sent me into a bit of a tailspin. There were many more court appearances, on visitation details and financial terms.

Publicly, and with my girls, I took the high road. Privately, I stewed in anger. Two things kept me going: work, and my relationship with Denyce, whom I had known since 1981. In fairly short order, we moved in together, got married, had a child of our own—Kayla, born in 1999—and went about the messy, joyous, exhausting business of raising a blended family (Denyce had a twelve-year-old boy named Corey from a previous relationship). To varying degrees, I was now responsible for five children. There was no time for self-pity or legal analysis about the efficacy and fairness of the family court system.

I had a job to do.

It's interesting, though, to examine the ways in which my opinion on child-rearing and family have changed over the years. In the heat of a custody battle, I was 100 percent convinced that I was the superior parent and that my daughters would have been better off with me; that, in fact, they really didn't even need their mother. I could do it all. This was hubris. It was also wrong. The fact that I had grown up without a father left me with a chip on my shoulder in many aspects of life: college, law school, work, family. I would do it all and lay waste to the doubters. But if not for Denyce's support during my custody dispute, I would not even have had a case. She had allowed me to continue working crazy hours and providing a stable home environment. And she did it while working a demanding executive job for UPS.

Similarly, as my daughters grew up, and we all managed to navigate the muddy waters of co-parenting, the anger receded, replaced by a shared commitment to do what was right for the children, all of whom I've had the honor to watch mature into well-adjusted and successful young adults. It became ever clearer to me that children need two parents, both a mother and father, regardless of whether the parents are married, divorced, separated. And while it might be an antiquated notion, I'll say this as well: girls, in particular, need a mother. And boys, in particular, need a father.

Chapter 13

OFF TO SEATTLE

"**W**e gotta figure out a way to stop this."

In the late 1990s, the digital revolution pushed the music business into a state of flux. And here was Tony Dofat, sitting in my office, apoplectic, talking about how to stop Napster and other platforms from taking the legs out from under the traditional recording industry.

I shook my head. "If they're already doing it, then it's too late. Cat's out of the bag. I don't care if you start suing people, you're never going back to the old model. It's over."

In fact, lawsuits, spearheaded by Metallica and others, the chosen mode of defense in those early days of the digital music onslaught, only served to embolden consumers and publicize their cause. *Free music for everyone!* won the day.

These were terrifying times for artists and industry executives alike. A decades-old business model had been built on the premise that recorded music was a salable commodity. Artists would put out a record and then embark on a promotional tour to support that record. A significant portion of a musician's income (and the income of the label that supported the artist) was derived from the sale of a physical product: recorded albums (or singles), either in vinyl, cassette, or compact disc. Suddenly, that model was flipped on its head . . . and still is. Artists earn a comparative pittance from downloads or streams, and most of their revenue is derived from touring, or from monetizing social media accounts whose numbers are bolstered by a song's popularity. (Publicly, Spotify has stated that it pays artists between $.003 and $.005 per stream. Translation: 250 streams will result in revenue of approximately one dollar for the recording artist.)

Thus, the music itself has been turned primarily into a marketing tool used to entice listeners to the product: concert and festival tickets, and a social media advertising platform. It is a much tougher and leaner business model. Additionally, it is a model that changed the notion that record labels and producers needed only one decent track around which they could build an entire album. This happened all the time in the vinyl era: an artist came up with a hit single, an album was quickly assembled, often with filler that did not meet the standard established by the single. Streaming platforms changed all of that. Consumers today seek out only the individual songs they like, and do it for a fraction of what they used to spend on albums. Ten bucks a month gets you access to thousands of songs on Spotify or Pandora or Apple Music roughly the same amount a single album cost in the pre-streaming era. For consumers, it has been a landmark victory (except for the part about artists not being able to create art if they can't feed themselves); for artists and record labels, it has been a catastrophic blow.

For everyone connected to the music business, it was a shock to the system. For me, it was provocation to consider what I wanted to do with the next phase of my career. In early 2000, I received a call from a corporate recruiter about a position with Microsoft, which was looking for an in-house counsel with a background in entertainment law—specifically, to work in the company's burgeoning digital media division. The job would entail working with content providers and negotiating deals in which they would agree to make their content—music, movies, television shows, books—available to consumers via Microsoft's Windows Media Player. In a sense, I would still be in the entertainment business; I would be spending a lot of time working with the same recording industry executives with whom I had built prior relationships.

But there were downsides, as well. For one thing, I was recently married, with a one-year-old baby and a stepson, living in a nice place in the New York City suburbs. I wasn't eager to leave them—or my other daughters—three thousand miles behind while I moved to Microsoft's headquarters in the Pacific Northwest. From an experience standpoint, though, it was almost too good an offer to turn down.

Deeply conflicted and at a crossroads in my career, I solicited advice from friends and colleagues, including, most notably, Clarence Avant. If I had to name one person who has been the most important mentor in my life, it would be Clarence, "the Black Godfather." In an extraordinary life that now spans almost ninety years, Clarence has been among the most influential men in Black culture, music, politics, and civil rights. It's no surprise that Netflix's documentary on Clarence featured interviews with not just a who's who of music and entertainment industry superstars, but also former US presidents Barack Obama and Bill Clinton.

In the early 1990s, Clarence became chairman of the board of Motown Records. As lofty a title as that might be, it denotes only a fraction of the wisdom and power he wielded. When the offer came down from Microsoft, I consulted with Clarence. Would I be making a mistake, I wondered, by leaving the music business and walking away from a firm I had started? Clarence talked me through the pros and cons, but in the end, he offered a steely assessment, in a way that only Clarence could.

"Son, take your ass to Microsoft, and get some of that stock."

I didn't accept Microsoft's offer right away. I wrestled with the decision for a few months, and even after I took the job, I repeatedly delayed the start date, in part to wrap up loose ends with my legal practice but also because I was reluctant to leave. I was again faced with a question of choice between the personal and the professional, one I had failed before with Tania. I was also being forced to confront a personal regret, one that I knew would test my relationship with Denyce like none other.

A few years prior, she had been presented with a similar choice of her own—one that would have significantly advanced her pay and responsibility but also pulled us hundreds of miles away, to South Carolina. She really wanted to take the job.

I could have moved my practice. I could have made sure I flew home to visit my daughters. I could have made the sacrifice so that Denyce could accept the job, the kind that did not often present itself to Black women. But I was in the midst of a seemingly limitless upward curve at the time with my entertainment business, and I must have known in my heart Denyce would not want to go without me. She declined the job, pretended it didn't bother her, and life—on the surface at least—went on. We got married, had a baby (Denyce's son, Corey, also lived with us), and I kept bumping up the pace on the treadmill. Fast-forward a couple years, and I'm on the phone with a recruiter discussing a new job with Microsoft, one that would take me farther away than the few hundred miles that had impeded my support for my wife's opportunity. Worse still, I didn't grant Denyce, my then-newlywed wife, much in the way of choice in the Microsoft matter. I hemmed and hawed privately until it was almost time to go. I wrestled with the weight of my convictions and my past, the promises made to those who'd helped thrust me out of poverty and crime, the clients who still looked to me for the same kind of help I'd once gotten myself. By the time I'd finally worked the choice out in my mind, there was almost no room for negotiation.

I'm going for approximately a year, and I think you and Corey and the baby should stay.

The pretense was one of generosity and practicality, but really, I was scared of bringing along the potential distraction of uprooting my family while hoping to settle into a life-changing new career path. I wanted to be able to focus on work, and I truly did not think Denyce wanted to move anyway—we had a new baby, a son in middle school, and she was coping with some health issues. Moreover, I felt, in the back of my mind, that this might be only a temporary gig—that I would spend a year working for Microsoft and return to New York armed with cutting-edge knowledge about the industry that would give me an advantage when, inevitably, I reentered the world of entertainment law. But the point is, I had used the sequencing of events to leave Denyce without a choice. Separation, we learned, is not good for a marriage, or any relationship, for that matter. Physical distance can lead to emotional distance, and eventually to both partners naturally leading separate and independent lives. While I traveled between Seattle and New York with some regularity, it wasn't the same as living together, sharing meals each evening, waking up next to each other in bed, watching television with the kids.

I had one life in the Pacific Northwest; she had another life in New York. I thought it would work. It didn't. Turning down the job and remaining in New York would have been better for my marriage. Taking the job was better for my career. Sometimes I regret that decision. I've heard it's possible to reconcile those choices and find a way to make it all function seamlessly. But in my case, in a time before routine video calls and easy telecommunication, the differences were irreconcilable. I can't speak to anyone else's choices with regard to the personal matters of love and family. But I made mine, informed perhaps by that survivor's mentality developed at the Amsterdam Houses—I wear my choices now and always will, an asterisk on the story I couldn't, and wouldn't, dare leave out.

Frankly, my two years in Seattle were lonely and isolating. After a lifetime living in New York and Washington,

DC, Seattle felt like the whitest city on earth, and Microsoft reflected that lack of diversity. Roughly 3 percent of the company's workforce then was African American; I was the third Black counsel ever hired at the company and one of the others had left by the time I arrived, leaving just two of us behind.

Compounding this issue was my decision to live in suburban Redmond, right across the street from the Microsoft campus. If Seattle was 6 percent African American (approximately the case in the early 2000s), then Redmond was less than 1. But I figured if I stayed next to the campus, there would be no distractions, and that certainly proved to be the case. I worked twelve-hour days, often six and sometimes seven days a week. It paid off. We began closing deals with book publishers, movie studios, and music labels, and business boomed. At one point early in the transition, my supervisor came into my office and sheepishly asked how I was doing. It wasn't a work question. It was a personal question. She seemed uncomfortable.

"I'm doing fine," I said. "Thank you for asking. But the truth is, I've been doing this my whole life—figuring out how to get along in a roomful of white folks. I'm used to it. Maybe you should be asking them how they're doing, since most of them have never worked with a Black man before."

She smiled. "Okay. Fair enough."

Maybe it was the clothes that tipped her off. In New York I had worked in a thriving creative environment, with artists and musicians, as well as attorneys. Outside of record industry executives, most of my colleagues and clients—and even many of my adversaries—were African American. Microsoft was a much quieter, more conservative, and yes, whiter, corporate climate. But here's the interesting thing: the dress code at Microsoft was far more relaxed.

The dress code I had imposed on myself in New York— dark suits, white or blue shirts, understated ties—was out of step with the attire at Microsoft. Even in the legal department, men wore khakis and polo shirts or golf shirts. I felt like I had entered a country club, and everyone else was waiting to tee off.

For a while, no one said anything. Every day I'd put on a suit and go to work, a Black guy wearing Giorgio Armani, Hugo Boss, and Valentino surrounded by a legion of white folks straight out of a Gap commercial. When it became apparent that I was not going to pick up the memo, they started teasing me.

"Looking sharp, Bruce. You have a job interview today or something?"

Or . . .

"Sorry for your loss, Bruce."

Finally, I gave in and adopted the Microsoft uniform; I did it all in a single weekend, went out and bought a dozen pairs of khaki pants in an array of colors, with golf shirts and polo shirts to match. The suits went in the back of the closet; for the most part, they stayed there for the next two years.

I treated my time in Seattle like a college experience, minus the fun part (which, come to think of it, was a lot like my original college experience). I was there to work, to learn. My entire life, it seemed, was distilled to those two things.

At the office holiday party that first year, I was presented with two gag gifts: a pillow and an ironing board.

"You spend all your time in the office," someone said. "Might as well make it a little easier."

There was a lot I didn't understand, from technology to terminology to social mores. One day a message began circulating around the office, announcing an upcoming "ship party." I had no idea what this meant, but it sounded pretty great, like the company was going to spring for a yacht and hors d'oeuvres. Why they were going to do this, I had no idea. But, hey, it was Microsoft, money was flowing. And maybe this Gates fellow, I figured, was a cool guy, an enlightened leader who understood the importance of keeping the troops happy.

By the end of the day, I had decided to ask for details. Would we be cruising around Puget Sound? Tethered to the dock on the waterfront? It sounded like the kind of thing that might have occurred in the music industry, where money was frequently thrown around with abandon.

"So, what's the deal with this *ship party?*" I asked a colleague. "That like a moonlight cruise on the bay?"

He laughed, softly at first, then harder, the kind of long, sustained belly laugh that instantly makes you realize you've said something stupid.

"Yeah . . . Hahaha . . . not that kind of ship, Bruce," he said, trying to catch his breath.

"What do you mean?" I could feel the embarrassment rising in my throat.

"It's a verb, not a noun. Whenever we launch a new product—whenever we *ship* it—we have a little event in the office to celebrate the occasion."

"Oh."

His laugh by now had been reduced to a mere smile—I think he was embarrassed by my embarrassment and felt bad for me.

"Hey, don't worry about it," he said. "Sometimes, in the tech world, we speak a different language. You'll be fluent in no time."

I was not fluent in no time, but eventually, with a lot of work and practice and repeated exposure, I did become comfortable and conversational in the language of technology, at least as it pertained to digital content. Comfort around the office, however, was slow to come, friendships difficult to acquire and maintain. I was homesick not just for the company of other Black people but also for the warmth and familiarity that comes with being around friends and family, people you've known a long time. A subtler sense of otherness was provoked by the fact that I wasn't merely a Black man but a Black man from the Northeast. And not just the Northeast, but New York, a city at once the most diverse and provincial of all. When viewed from Seattle, I came to realize, New York might as well have been on a different planet, either maligned or misunderstood. I expected Microsoft, as a world leader in technology, to boast a diverse, international workforce. And while that has certainly become a much more accurate description today, it was not really the case twenty years ago. The vast majority of my colleagues in the legal department—nearly all of them, in fact—were not just white but also local. It felt like most were raised in the Pacific Northwest, with a smattering of Californians mixed in. An exception was my manager, an Italian woman from the Bronx, with whom I could at least joke about the Yankees. But she had a family and friends. She had a life.

My world was three thousand miles away.

The work was hard and interesting and required the flexing of muscles I hadn't used in a while—the kind involved in breaking down a new and complex task into elements more familiar and understandable. By the time I joined Microsoft, I had become quite proficient in the writing and negotiation of contracts, both for artists and industry executives. I wouldn't say the job was boring, but it had become somewhat repetitive, as is the case with any job you've done for a while. That, combined with the cratering of artists' royalties and industry revenue overall, made the Microsoft job appealing. It was different and potentially more lucrative, but there was a learning curve, the riding of which prompted anxiety on a level I hadn't experienced in some time.

It's always challenging to start a new job, but the truth is, as a Black person in corporate America, it was doubly hard. To function inside what remains a predominantly white, male ecosystem, you are held to a different standard. That is simply a fact. I am obligated to present well at all times; there is no margin for error. The crushing weight of expectation, of carrying the hopes and opportunities of future African American professionals on your shoulders, can be daunting, as can the presumption in some corners that you were hired precisely because of your ethnicity, rather than in spite of your ethnicity, or without regard to your ethnicity. You are a quota . . . an attempt at *diversity and inclusion,* words that have somehow been twisted into pejoratives by traditional, often fearful and defensive white society, which wants nothing more than to maintain the status quo. I felt the pressure at Hofstra and Georgetown, and especially at Silverstein and Mullens. I felt it when we were building the most successful African American entertainment law firm in the country.

And I felt it when I got to Microsoft.

If I screwed up, I could lose my career. Just as important, my missteps could impact the opportunities for other Black professionals following in my footsteps, and especially for other Black attorneys at Microsoft. That responsibility was never far from the front of my brain, and I vowed that wherever my career took me, I would do my best to not merely lead by example—through hard work and professionalism—but to make a concerted effort to open doors for others who came after me. Even if it pissed some people off, which of course it would.

Assimilation is a complex term, implying both the positive aspects of working within a group to achieve a common goal, and the negative connotation of subjugating one's beliefs or desires—however mundane or important—to placate others. I had come from a small company in which I was one of the founders and partners—a company comprised entirely of people of color, working in an aggressive, confrontational field historically dominated by Caucasians. My personality was a natural fit for the daily sparring of entertainment law; less so for the more restrained corporate atmosphere of Microsoft.

I was determined to fit in without losing myself, but I very quickly developed a reputation as someone who would speak his mind on almost any subject, and in conversation with any colleague, from one of my assistants all the way up to the president. I had been this way my entire life, and I wasn't about to change simply because I was working for Microsoft. Not to say that I was antagonistic or impolite, but I did not shy away from awkward or uncomfortable conversations, including those centered around race. I had been hired because of my legal expertise and extensive contacts within the music business, but I was also part of the company's new diversity initiative. There's no getting around that. And there were days when I felt the pressure to not just fit in and do my job well, but once again to be a standard bearer for Black attorneys and for Black professionals in corporate America.

Over the years, I have come to realize how fortunate I am to have the support of Microsoft in furthering this initiative, but in the beginning, as I wrestled with homesickness and loneliness and a persistent feeling of otherness, there were some difficult days. Would I classify this as being a result of racism? Well, certainly not in the obvious manner I had encountered in previous phases of my life: college, law school, internships . . . even when I first entered the music business. It was subtler, perhaps owing to cultural differences between the Northeast and the Pacific Northwest. I had spent my entire life in the I-95 corridor between DC and New York, where people for the most part tell you exactly how they feel. No matter how uncomfortable it might be. In Seattle, I realized, people generally kept their feelings to themselves. Not necessarily a bad thing or a good thing—it was just a different experience.

True diversity involves reaching across professional, social, and cultural divides, breaking out of your comfort zone. I had been doing this my whole life. When I arrived at

Microsoft, I got the sense that this was a foreign concept. Not once in those early days did a colleague invite me to their home. There was one client, a white guy, who had a nice boat docked on Lake Washington, and one day we spent a few hours riding around and talking. That was nice, and I appreciated him going out of his way to make it happen. But he was a client, not a coworker. The people with whom I worked every day? They were cordial, polite, distant. Most likely they were simply not comfortable around me. We were undeniably different—not just ethnically, but geographically, culturally, professionally, and personally.

I did my thing, and they did theirs. My thing mainly involved working ridiculously long days and going home at night to a sterile corporate apartment. Theirs involved . . . well . . . I don't know. More than a few had families. They all had friends and social networks and hobbies. Whatever they did in their off-hours, I was not invited. Obviously, there was no obligation to include the new guy, or to try to make him feel at home. Occasional trips to Los Angeles or New York, where I not only spent time with my wife and kids but also reconnected with former colleagues in the music industry, provided a respite, but they also served to reinforce the feelings of isolation in Seattle.

Again, this is not racism in the sense typically reserved for the word, but it is part of the discussion when we are talking about diversity and inclusion. Microsoft at the dawn of the century was a company experiencing vast growth and change, and it was to their credit that they were at least taking steps toward diversifying their workforce at all levels. But the legal department was neither diverse nor inclusive at that time. Most of my colleagues were quiet professionals who likely thought they were being inclusive by saying hello to me in the cafeteria. Management probably thought it was a sign of inclusion that a Ping-Pong table had been installed in the break room. But these were merely gestures of tolerance, not inclusion.

Diversity happens mostly at the recruitment and hiring stage, and it is crucial; but it is, in many ways, merely a prerequisite for the intensely hard work of inclusion. To diversify a workforce (or, for example, a college population) by increasing representation among men and women of color (or of any traditionally underrepresented community) does little without making those new team members feel welcome in the new environment. I'm sure that, if pressed, most of my colleagues would have strongly denied any racist tendencies whatsoever and defaulted to *Hey, I got my life, and Bruce has his life.* That's true. We were under no obligation to interact socially outside the office. But I've learned, through my professional work in the arena, that collegiality and humanity can be fostered with hard work.

The loneliness took its toll. One night, maybe a year into my tenure, I went to a gospel performance at a nearby church, just to experience what I hoped would be a connection with both music and other people of color. Indeed, during my time in Seattle, this was the largest contingent of Black people I'd seen in a single place. There was just one problem: most of them were at least a generation older than me. I remember looking around as people sang and held hands. They smiled and threw their heads back and sang joyfully with their friends and fellow congregants; I imagined they had known each other forever. And so even here, in a Black church, I felt out of place.

I was deeply discouraged by the experience—it had felt like a long shot perhaps, a last grasp at finding community in an unfamiliar territory, but this outcome was almost unbearable. I couldn't help but think for a moment that I had made a poor decision in managing my career. Not so long ago, I had been representing some of the top artists in music, I was sitting in on recording sessions with platinum-selling artists and soaking up the energy just offstage at packed venues around the country. And now, on a Saturday night, here I was, so desperate for connection that I'd resorted to an amateur church performance in a crowd old enough to host my parents—or grandparents.

There had to be more to life.

Chapter 14

WE CAN DO BETTER

Near the two-year mark in Seattle, I tried joining some colleagues on a sojourn to a local nightclub. I had managed to strike up some acquaintances here and there through the job, and a handful of young associates, mostly women, all white, from a firm with which we had conducted considerable business, had been trying for a while to get me to join them for drinks after work. I always declined, but they knew I was lonely and continued to push. Their efforts came from a place of generosity, and I appreciated that, so after turning down a dozen invitations, I finally accepted. To say I had no idea what I was getting into would be an understatement.

This was Seattle, the birthplace of grunge, in the early 2000s, so of course the downtown club was stuffed to the rafters with white folks in flannel, bobbing their heads to Nirvana, Soundgarden, and Pearl Jam covers. I walked into that joint, feeling like the Blackest man in America, and joined the inviting group's table. There were four of us. I was the only male. I put my hands in my lap and tried not to move a muscle. I looked at my watch, tried to figure out how quickly I could leave without being disrespectful.

One drink became two, two became three, and the inhibitions started to drift away.

"Come on, Bruce!" one of the attorneys said, as she shimmied toward the dance floor, hand extended.

I looked around, couldn't believe what I was seeing, or that I was part of it.

"Uh-uh. I'm good," I shouted over the music.

She moved closer, took me by the arm, and pulled me out of my seat. "Don't be afraid to have fun!"

Sister, that is not what I'm afraid of. Believe me.

The next thing I knew, I was out on the dance floor. Except no one was dancing—at least not any kind of dancing I recognized. They were just . . . *jumping.* Bouncing into the air like a pod of dolphins, shaking from side to side, craning their necks, and then thudding to the floor. Over and over. And there I was, right alongside them.

A thought flashed through my mind, laser-like, filled with shame.

Oh, Lord . . . if anyone back home could see me right now.

I woke the next day with a thundering hangover, not so much from the drinks but from the crushing effects of an anxious night—sleepless in Seattle once again. I showered, downed a few cups of coffee, and went into the office early. When my manager arrived, I walked straight into her office.

"Look," I began. "I want you to know that this is not a negotiation ploy. I need to go back home."

"Why?" she asked. "You're doing so well here."

"Thank you. I appreciate that. But I'm miserable. I miss my friends and my family, and there's just not enough diversity."

"We're working on that," she said. "It takes time."

"I know. I'm not just talking about Microsoft. It's the whole city."

"Give it some more time," she suggested. "Seattle will grow on you."

In my head I could see a loop of the previous night's revelry, staccato images flashing across my mind's eye—a roomful of unfamiliar people jumping up and down, fists clenched, sweat flying, indecipherable music blaring in the background.

And there I was, in the middle of the melee, trying to fit in, a wave of something akin to shame washing over me.

I blinked away the memory.

"I appreciate your support," I said. "I really do. But I've given this a lot of thought, and I think it's best that I move on."

This pronouncement led quickly to an intervention from Brad Smith, who had recently been named Microsoft's general counsel. In the years since, Brad and I have become very close. He is a trusted friend and colleague, and also, as I have discovered, deeply committed to the issues of diversity and inclusion. Brad offered to help me find a position within the company that might be more suitable. He first suggested a music policy job in DC, which I politely declined because, well, it wasn't New York. Then he suggested a job working in anti-piracy law in New York. That didn't interest me from a legal standpoint.

Finally, Brad said, "How about sales?"

And that was it.

I moved to Microsoft's offices in New York and began working as a counsel supporting sales in the East Region. I loved the work, and I was happy to be home. There were promotions, salary increases. Eventually, I was supporting the entire US sales team, as part of a $20 billion business. And the new position granted me more opportunity to help expand Microsoft's efforts on diversity, inclusion, and mentorship. New York was a bigger playground, so to speak, and I was able to meet a lot of people involved in diversity efforts, both inside and outside the company. It was also easier to recruit talent. Improvement and progress came not just through formal programs instituted in the early years of the twenty-first century but through legitimate company-wide commitment to results, not merely lip service.

That was so important to me, because at heart I'm still that ten-year-old kid handcuffed to a chair in a Brooklyn police precinct. I'm still the young intern at a swanky luncheon at the George Town Club, being asked to describe life in the ghetto. A couple years after I moved back to New York, I was encouraged by a meeting with Brad, in which he repeated his desire to transform Microsoft into a workplace truly committed to diversity and inclusion.

"We can do better," he said. "I know that."

By that point in my career, I was routinely taking calls from colleagues, or friends of colleagues, inquiring about job opportunities—not only at Microsoft, but throughout the legal profession, or even in the music industry. If I respected the person's work but they had no desire to move to Seattle, I'd recommend them to another company. Sometimes I played the role of recruiter, pursuing attorneys who were working in entertainment law and trying to convince them to consider an in-house position with Microsoft. I knew from experience that many attorneys viewed the move to in-house counsel suspiciously—as if it represented some sort of surrender or sellout. Or even complacency. Most lawyers enjoy working with a multitude of clients, and those who own their firms are usually reluctant to give up the power and control that comes with being at the top of the masthead. I was the same way. Until I wasn't.

Sure, it took me a few years to stop craving the rush of adrenaline that came with representing high-profile clients in the entertainment industry, but once established, I began to see the benefits: a similarly demanding professional and intellectual environment; a stable position with a lucrative compensation and benefits package; the chance to move vertically; and, perhaps most important of all, the chance to be of service to other men and women of color seeking inroads into American corporate culture.

If Brad were merely paying lip service, I probably would have left. But I was convinced, through action, that he walked the walk. And actions not merely to benefit Microsoft, either. We were empowered to push bigger, broader change with the company's platform as an accelerator. In the early 2000s, I became part of the National Association of Minority and Women Owned Law Firms, the stated mission of which is to "promote diversity in the legal profession by fostering successful relationships among preeminent minority and women owned law firms and private/public entities." Microsoft was one of the founding members of that organization, but my involvement was not tied explicitly to recruiting talented attorneys to Microsoft (although that sometimes was the end result). The primary goal of the organization was, simply, to encourage corporations to hire both women and professionals of color on an individual basis, and to promote relationships between those corporations and law firms owned by minorities and women.

I thought back to my own tribulations as a young Black law school graduate who had less access to the face-to-face social opportunities that often preface a job offer, and I pushed to organize the first Corporate, External, and Legal Affairs (CELA) Women and Minority Law Student Intellectual Property Summit in New York. It would be, we assured, a very big tent. And to prove it, we secured the involvement of some of the biggest tech giants of the time, including Sun Microsystems, IBM, Google, and others. All competitors of ours, but in this case, we all had a common goal and a common interest.

The first event was a rousing success, attracting hundreds of students (predominantly law school students, but some undergraduate students as well), most from the New York metropolitan area, but some from Philadelphia, DC, and other eastern cities. It has evolved over the years to include participation from many traditional law firms, as well as the tech companies. No longer could white-shoe firms lament the supposed paucity of minority talent in the law school ranks, claiming commitment to the cause of diverse hiring with the caveat "if we could find them."

I was in a position to put truth to this lie. I was that Black attorney who started out as one outlier in a sea of white faces at a boutique firm. It was not a great experience, but I'll say this: They found me. And I found them. It wasn't that difficult.

"You can't find the talent?" I reasoned. "Fine, then we'll bring the talent to you. All you have to do is show up." With no shortage of candidates on hand, and an unignorable corporate backer and participant list, this excuse, at least, was finally on its way out.

Best of all, the IP summit wasn't a one-off. At Microsoft, we were establishing a culture wherein every job opening is treated as an opportunity to diversify the workplace—and showing what that means: making sure the pool of applicants is heterogenous and giving every person on the slate an equal opportunity to win the job. We were conducting community outreach with projects such as the Elevate America Community Initiative, which provided free technology training to underserved communities in New York, and, in 2011, funded a $250,000 grant to the Henry Street Settlement's Workforce Development Center for technology training, job placement, childcare, and transportation to women, disadvantaged young adults, and homeless individuals facing barriers to employment and re-employment.

I'm proud to have helped establish a culture that prizes diversity in its legal department, but we need people who are skilled in an array of disciplines, most notably computer science and engineering. It's crucial that we reach young people and help them understand and become proficient in our technology so that one day they will enter and strengthen the pool of candidates who might want to work in our industry. And we will want to hire them. A kid growing up in poverty, attending underfunded schools, has a far steeper hill to climb. If we can make that journey a bit more manageable, this will be worth it.

And we also worked to make these issues accessible and relevant to the communities being targeted for help. Microsoft donated $5 million to the founding of the Universal Hip Hop Museum (UHHM) in the Bronx, as part of its Artificial Intelligence for Cultural Heritage program. Through this partnership, Microsoft, as the official technology partner of the UHHM, became a benefactor committed to preserving the history of hip hop and facilitating a better understanding and appreciation of its cultural impact—particularly among youth.

All of this is vitally important to me, personally. I've seen too many outreach programs pitched nowhere to nobody, too many initiatives—even well-meaning ones—woefully underfunded or out of touch. I enjoy little more than speaking to elementary and high school students, spreading the gospel of hope and optimism in the face of challenges. This is the stuff that motivates me now, that gets me out of bed in the morning. Closing deals is a rush. Don't get me wrong. But knowing that I might play some small part in the development of children from underserved communities who will one day close even bigger deals? Hard to put a value on that.

It's fine to *talk* about diversity and inclusion, but at the end of the day, what matters is the results. We all like the good noise of diversity lunches and symposia, but here's what we need to ask: How many diverse candidates do you have working for your company? How many people of color? How many women? How many people from the LGBTQ+ community? Let's review your organizational charts. Look around your own company and tell me what you see.

For me, this has always been a priority. My team at Microsoft was made up of twenty-four people. Of those, fifteen were women. Of those fifteen women, seven were African American. We also had two Asian men, two Latino men, three African American men, and two Caucasian men—all supporting a $20 billion business. I could quote sales figures and contract numbers for hours, but there is no statistic related to my time at Microsoft that makes me prouder than those diversity numbers. I am fortunate and grateful to have forged lasting friendships with individuals like Brad Smith, who became the company's president during this build-out and was so thoroughly and openly committed to supporting the cause, and executives like Neal Suggs and Fred Humphries, who have provided guidance and mentorship in the cause for expanding my company's commitment to diversity.

Diversity is not about quotas or exclusion. It's not about refusing to hire white candidates. It's about ensuring that diverse candidates are given a fair opportunity. It's about making sure that there is a woman or a minority candidate for every position, and not in name only. You don't just put them on the slate for the sake of appearances. You present them with a real chance to win the job. After winning Microsoft's diversity award, I actually got up and gave a speech to that effect to an overwhelmingly positive response:

"Be brave. Be courageous. Don't be afraid of change. It's perfectly acceptable for you to hire more than one person with a diverse background. If there's more than one diverse candidate that deserves a job, then hire two. Or five! It's okay!"

Brad, looking on, smiled. I knew he had my back.

I hope the young people I connect with as a mentor and advocate can look at me and see that almost anything is possible, that you don't have to be a victim of circumstances and surroundings. That life deals a shitty hand sometimes, and it's okay to be angry about that, but that anger can be utilized in a productive way. I am living proof that you can transcend your environment, without an athletic scholarship or a record deal.

But I also tell them there are no shortcuts, that they will have to work their butts off, and that at every important juncture in their lives, someone will question their aptitude and commitment because of assumptions based primarily on their appearance or history. That you'll have to prove yourself. And then you'll have to prove yourself again. Because there is a presumption that you're just not worthy. You're a kid from the projects. You're not good enough. Well . . . prove them wrong.

I've always believed that whatever I've gone through, whatever experience I have endured, there is value to it. Whether it's selling stolen newspapers, opening taxi doors, or getting profiled by law enforcement, it's all part of who I am. The little struggles prepare you for the big struggles—in life, and in corporate America. Embrace your past. Don't run from it. Not everyone is like that. I know people, even at Microsoft, who want to hide their deepest selves. I've called a few out on it.

Your grandmother is on public assistance? Or your mom? Maybe a brother or sister? An uncle or a cousin? But you don't want anyone to know. You want to play that role during the day at work, fine. But when you come home, or it's just you and me talking, let's be honest. Don't carry that lie into a social environment—not with me, because I don't have the tolerance for that. By talking about our roots, by exploring and acknowledging our commonality, we give others hope. We let them know there is nothing to be ashamed of, and in the process, perhaps, normalize empathy and aid. So, please, don't hide the truth of your life from me.

I know where you're from; I'm from the same place.

Chapter 15

HOME AGAIN

With distance, I can see how strange it must have seemed to those around me: The well-compensated attorney for Microsoft coming home to the Amsterdam Houses projects every night. From the outside, I looked like a lottery winner, so why in the hell was I sleeping in the same bed I had slept in as a child?

I had returned to New York eager to start the new role and to reconnect with my wife and kids, but my marriage, frayed from my time in Seattle, continued to erode steadily over the next few years. Denyce and I had closed the physical distance, but the emotional fissure was as large as ever—thanks in no small part to my continued dedication to a life built around work.

There was an attempt, in 2006, at something of a warming. Denyce, at my daughter Kayla's request, planned a birthday party for me at our home in Mount Vernon. It was a backyard barbecue for a couple dozen people, with hot dogs, hamburgers, chicken, and salmon, and an abundance of salads and other side dishes, all enjoyed to a soundtrack of R&B

and rap. I was at the grill, cooking up a storm, when I noticed smoke coming from a basement window of the house. I ran to the back door and tried to enter the basement but was quickly overcome by a wall of smoke. Apparently, with everyone occupied by the revelry in the backyard, an electrical fire had sparked and grown unnoticed and unabated from the basement, spreading to the main floor, and then to the second. By the time the fire department arrived and began wrestling with an uncooperative fire hydrant, we were all standing out on the front lawn, watching smoke give way to flames.

The damage was substantial. What might have been a minor restoration project with quicker intervention became a yearlong rebuild, sending Denyce and our daughter to stay at a nearby hotel in New Rochelle (my stepson, Corey, was away at college).

I joined them only for the first night. The following day, seeking the easiest out at the time, I moved back into my mother's apartment at the Amsterdam Houses, a decision made ostensibly out of convenience—I'd be closer to the Microsoft Midtown offices—but it was also a quiet declaration: our marriage was over.

There was some counseling, mostly ineffective, but no deep discussion about reconciliation. There was no custody battle. Denyce kept the house in Mount Vernon and primary custody of our daughter. She was a terrific mom and had been a supportive partner. I shouldered most of the blame for the breakup. And yet, Denyce left a significant amount of money on the table during the divorce proceedings— money to which she was legally entitled, and the loss of which would have made my life even harder. When my attorney asked her why she was being so amicable, she replied simply, "We're friends. There's no reason why we have to become enemies."

For the better part of the next four years, I lived in the projects with my mother, mostly, yes, because of convenience—proximity to work, the support of family, a comfortable bed, and homecooked meals—but also to save a little money, and perhaps to remind myself, every day, that this was my home. This was the nest I had fled, but it would always be part of my life, part of what made me the man I became. Whenever I would go to a Microsoft black-tie event, usually around the holidays, friends in the projects would see me leaving and yell out the window.

"Where are you going, Bruce?"

I'd look up and smile.

"Disney World!"

A joke, sure, but in every joke, there is the residue of truth. Or deflection—an attempt to swat away the pain with laughter.

It was all so complicated, and to dwell on whatever hardships I might have been experiencing—the twin failed relationships and the financial challenges that went with them—and how they had put me in a place that seemed incongruous to the professional achievements I had attained, was both a colossal waste of time and a pointless exercise in self-flagellation. Simply put, I couldn't go there. Mentally, spiritually, economically, I couldn't afford to give it a second thought, let alone explain it to anyone else. You can't leave the Amsterdam Houses every morning, walk to work at Microsoft, and return to the projects every night, without acknowledging the weirdness of it all—the juxtaposition of drastically different worlds. But I lacked the energy or the inclination to analyze it. I was in survival mode, and so, as I had so many times throughout my life, I put my head down and focused on the task at hand, on putting one foot in front of the other and trying to get through each day.

I toggled between worlds to the best of my ability, almost reflexively, instinctively shedding one skin and donning another when I returned home in the evening after a long day in corporate America. I'd take off the khakis and polo shirt and put on jeans and sneakers. I didn't want to walk around the neighborhood looking like the guy who worked at Microsoft, even though this was true, and everyone knew it. But it was also important to fit in, to not encourage feelings of resentment.

How strange to be the other in the neighborhood where I had grown up—surrounded by people whose experiences were not unlike my own. But there it was, an unavoidable and ironic fact of my existence at that moment. I had spent most of my life trying to rise above the circumstances of my youth, to demonstrate value through titles and degrees.

To get away.

Now I was back . . . again. And rather than striving to prove that I was different from everyone else—that I was somehow *better*—I wanted to demonstrate commonality. Because I believed it in my heart.

I'm not special. I haven't changed. I'm the same old Bruce. I just got lucky.

For all the hard work and determination, things still could have turned out very differently. Returning to the Amsterdam

Houses to live with my mother, difficult though it might have been, grounded me, reconnected me with my origin story.

Most of my time was spent at the office; free time was devoted to helping my mother or visiting my kids. I had some work to do in that regard, and I tried hard to make up for lost time, taking my older girls on what we referred to as "date night" once a week, and coaching my younger daughter's soccer team. I'd buy them chocolate-covered strawberries and flowers, not only because it made them happy but also to set the bar high for any would-be suitors. There wasn't a lot of room left in the schedule for socializing with the neighbors or reconnecting with childhood friends. But you can't live in a place for nearly four years without becoming part of the fabric of the community, at least to some extent. There were block parties and summer cookouts, opportunities to get to know people who weren't around when I was younger and whose lives and stories were not dissimilar to what I had known three decades earlier.

Time seemed to have stood still in the projects. People came and went, but the parameters of their lives, shaped by race and circumstance and lineage, and especially by the crushing effects of poverty, barely shifted at all. Some of my friends had made it out of the projects; others had gotten out for a while but had returned. More than a few never left. One day I ran into Keith, one of my childhood buddies. We talked about old times, shared a few laughs, and then the conversation turned to sadder news: our friend Freddie, who lived in my building all those years ago, had gotten seriously into drugs. I knew this, had run into Freddie a few times and seen what the substances were doing to him. He was strung-out most of the time.

We both lamented the decline of our friend, as if resigned to the inevitable conclusion his story would reach. But there was more to it, in Keith's mind—a need to affix blame for his friend's situation.

"This is on James," he said, invoking a name we had both known since childhood—the same person who had rescued me from an agitated foot soldier in the stairwell when I returned to the projects after moving back to New York some twenty years earlier. James was still James, and he did what he did. We knew his business, but he was hardly the only option for potential customers. I pointed this out to Keith.

"Can't pin this on James," I said. "Freddie is a grown man. He made his own choices. We all do."

"Fuck that. Freddie is his friend," Keith said. "You don't get your friends hooked on drugs." He paced as he spoke, clenching his fists, his voice rising an octave with each sentence. "Seriously want to kill that motherfucker."

"Easy, man," I said, trying to speak calmly, as something told me this wasn't just idle ranting. "You need to stay out of it. I love Freddie, too, but this isn't your problem."

Keith shook his head. "Fucking disgusting."

Keith had a point. In the frequently twisted logic of the streets, there were things you could do and things you could not do, and neither were necessarily dictated by legality or the norms of a civilized society. If you wanted to use drugs, that was your choice. If you wanted to sell drugs, well, that was your choice as well, but potentially a more complicated one, with a much greater likelihood of fallout for those around you. You were, for example, significantly more likely to go to jail, or to be killed. But if those were the risks you were willing to take, so be it. What you didn't do— what I could never have done, had I fallen into that life way back when—is sell to your closest friends, especially if those friends had fallen down the rabbit hole of addiction, as Freddie clearly had.

To even entertain the notion that you could be the kind of person who sells drugs is to acknowledge something deep and dark within yourself. But if you grow up in the projects, surrounded by drugs and violence and poverty, it isn't such a stretch, and even now, so many years later, I could look at the situation through a different set of eyes.

"Everyone makes their own decisions," I said, referring to Freddie but also to Keith, who was teetering on the edge of a bad one. "Don't do anything stupid."

In time, Keith calmed down, wisely decided not to take matters into his own hands. Freddie got off drugs. James kept doing his thing. Life in the projects went on.

Eventually I got out again, to a place in West Orange, New Jersey. I lived there for a while, then bought a place in Brooklyn and moved there, this time taking in my mother to provide her an escape as well. Things began to fall into place, finally. I bought an apartment for my daughters, so that they could learn the basics of real estate investment and management when they got out of college, and enter the adult world on their feet, with a bit of security. I was grateful to have the resources to do all of this, to take care of my family and give them a better life.

And my relationship journey, the complications and obstacles, so many of which I've realized under examination were of my own creation, had fallen into a better place, too. God wasn't through with me yet. I was blessed to find Kat, a woman who helped make me a better partner, father, colleague, and friend.

But some things never change.

I got arrested, again.

Typically, I was careful about the type of music I would play in my car, especially in nice weather. The more genteel the neighborhood, the softer the music. But on this night, I was bumping some hip hop, and as I passed through Park Slope, one of those neighborhoods on my route home in Brooklyn, I was pulled over by the police.

Dammit, I thought. I'd given them an excuse to profile me.

They asked for the usual paperwork, and when it turned out I didn't have a physical copy of my insurance card in the glove compartment, the flashbacks began. There were two of them, one white, one Black. The white cop wanted to impound the car and bring me in, point-blank and with little room for thought. The car was insured, which they knew after running a vehicle ID check, but he was set on giving me a hard time. Fortunately, his partner talked him out of it, and I was allowed to leave with an admonishment to mail in a physical copy of the insurance card—a task I handled the very next day.

Maybe a week later, on a Saturday afternoon, I was stopped again, this time just a block from my house, on the way home from Trader Joe's. They gave no reason for pulling me over, just asked for my license and registration, but the infraction was all the same: I was a Black man driving a nice car in a gentrified neighborhood.

Must be a drug dealer.

I sat parked at the curb while the officers (both of whom were Caucasian) retreated to their car. Ten minutes passed. Twenty. Not a good sign. I called a cousin, who lived nearby, and asked him for help.

"Cops pulled me over," I explained. "Not sure what's going on, but I think they're going to take my car, and I need to get some stuff out of it."

More time passed. I waved out the window, inviting the officers to approach the car (I certainly wasn't going to get out, as that might have been construed as a confrontational act). After more than a half hour, they finally exited their vehicle.

"Sir, you're going to have to come with us," one of them said. "Something showed up on your license."

"Can you tell me what it is?"

"We don't have that information yet. It's an irregularity."

I tried to remain calm. "I'm entitled to know the legal reason for the stop."

"As I said, there's something on your license," he repeated. "Please empty your pockets and leave everything in the car."

And just like that, off I went, cast into the criminal justice system for the second time in less than a decade. First stop: the Sixty-Seventh Precinct, near the corner of Church and Nostrand. Handcuffed, stood for a mug shot, and then told to sit tight. Eventually, an officer explained that I was being held for driving an uninsured vehicle. Not true, I countered.

The vehicle was insured. I had sent in the physical card, per instructions, the previous week.

"Well, apparently it was never received," the officer said.

"That's not my problem."

He stared at me. "It is now."

Having been through this once before, you would think I would know better than to allow my mind to trail toward optimism. Nevertheless, I did not even bother to contact my attorney. I'd surely be out soon.

Instead, after stewing for a while, my name was called.

"Jackson! Let's go, you're going downtown to Central Booking."

The wash of déjà vu sent me scrambling.

"Do me a favor," I said on the drive over. "Make sure you put me in one of the holding cells that has a phone."

The cop raised an eye, surprised.

"Not a great idea. Those cells are usually packed. It's not the safest place."

"I'll be okay," I said. "I need to call my attorney."

He shrugged. "Suit yourself."

We walked through the buzzing passageway, overrun with cops and criminals and attorneys and judges, past a half dozen cells equipped with phones, each overflowing with inmates. The cop handed me off to a corrections officer, with the recommendation that I be put in one of the cells so that I could make a call. The CO, a big puffy white guy, laughed.

"Nah, that motherfucker's going in the back."

There was no reason to do this, other than to mess with me. But I was just a Black man behind bars, trying to not piss

off a big, hostile CO with a chip on his shoulder and, potentially, animus in his heart for a guy of my complexion.

I wound up in a cell at the rear of the complex, surrounded by guys behaving exactly as they would on the
street: smoking, screaming, openly consuming. The smell
was horrible, the noise deafening.

"Y'all need to shut the fuck up!" I finally yelled. Most of
them ignored me. A few others gave me a hard look and
laughed. The noise went on, but that little outburst had the
important effect of announcing that I wasn't scared (although
I was, a bit), and that I wouldn't be easily intimidated.
Mainly, I was just saddened and angered by the irony of my
circumstances: fifty-three years old, Georgetown Law School
graduate, successful attorney for Microsoft . . . incarcerated
without cause (again!), in a jail located not more than a mile
from where I was held as a ten-year-old falsely accused of
theft.

I'd lived a lifetime to move that mile.

I spent another miserable night in jail before being
released the next morning. The charges were later dismissed,
but the anger and ignominy remained. For a couple years, I
kept the incident mostly to myself. Then, one day at work,
we got into a big discussion about diversity and systemic racism. Nerves were raw, and the emotions around the conversation had begun to rise. I told the story of a "friend," a
middle-aged Black professional in an expensive car who was
profiled and pulled over by police, and how he ended up
jailed for the heinous crime of driving a verifiably insured
vehicle without the physical documentation on hand. A lot

of my colleagues shook their heads in dismay; a few found the story apocryphal.

"Come on, Bruce. A little over the top, isn't it?"

Then, the big reveal. "No, it happened to me."

Jaws dropped around the table.

No shit?

"Listen," I began. "My world is different than your world once we leave this place. That's what some of you don't understand; hopefully you understand it now. There are thousands of stories like that every weekend. I just happen to be sitting here with you right now to tell it."

I paused.

"Please . . . let's never forget that."

I can look back now and draw a line between the little boy who used to run around the neighborhood in tattered cutoffs, with a latchkey dangling from his neck, and the grown man in his business suit, and see all the dots connected along the way—all the people who nudged me in the right direction, who wouldn't let me quit.

And I want to do the same. Each of us who has achieved some level of success has an obligation to reach out and lend a hand . . . to help coax the next generation of leaders forward. The older I get, the more I want to give back. I want to continue to be a mentor, and to help provide more opportunities for young people from disadvantaged backgrounds. We live in a world that is too often cold and cruel, and where a single gesture of kindness or generosity can make all the difference. I know. I worked hard. I made mostly good choices. But I was lucky, too, in a hundred different ways.

In a society obsessed with celebrity culture and social media, I worry young people have come to see the trappings of fame and fortune separate and apart from the work required to achieve success. It all seems so easy and attainable in an attention economy where "followers" and "likes" and "views" have become in and of themselves a measure of success, rather than a reflection of achievements elsewhere. To become a person of influence—literally, an *influencer*—is not a career plan; it's like planning to hit the lottery. There's little skill involved. Just randomness and luck. And maybe good bone structure. Young Black people, who have historically been denied opportunity, and whose life circumstances often are desperate, are particularly susceptible to the allure of luxury attained quickly at a young age, and the implicit promise of a transformative life.

There are, of course, celebrities who achieve remarkable success through talent and ambition and diligence. We see them all the time: the musicians, athletes, and actors. But for every kid who makes it to the NBA, there are a million others who never rise above the ranks of varsity-squad bench-rider. In fairness to the NBA, it is one of the most progressive and socially conscious organizations in professional sports. My "league," the American Bar Association, by contrast, lags woefully far behind many peer organizations when it comes to integration.

Nevertheless, the fact remains that there are far more lawyers in the world than there are professional basketball players, and an increasing number of opportunities, thanks partly to companies like Microsoft, led by people like Brad Smith, that do embrace a commitment to diversity and inclusion. It's okay to chase dreams, to set the bar high. But there are other avenues to success where the odds aren't so long, and where you can maintain a degree of control over your own destiny. You can work your ass off and change the course of not only your life but the lives of your entire family. If you work hard and access all the resources at your disposal (yes, there will be times when it seems as though those resources are lacking), you can secure a job to be proud of, a circle of friends and colleagues, and a comfortable existence for yourself and your family.

That might be a dream, but it's not a fantasy. There is a difference.

I'll speak sometimes in a school setting, or at a boys and girls' club, and I can tell by the look on the kids' faces that they view me as an outsider. The fact that I am African American is almost irrelevant to them. They are poor. I am wealthy. What could we possibly have in common? And I'll try to explain. I don't just understand you. I *was* you. I know what it's like to grow up with a mostly absent father. I know how it feels to see your friends die. I know the fear and indignity of sitting in a police station, handcuffed to a chair, while being interrogated and coerced into nearly admitting you did something that you did not do.

What I tell these kids is that mine is a story about persistence and hope, about overcoming the obstacles that life puts in our path. You can run through them or walk around them, and either approach can be painful. Physically painful, mentally painful, emotionally painful. But you can't stop at every roadblock. If you want to move forward in life, there's no option: you've got to keep moving. One path takes a little longer, but it doesn't mean it's the better or worse way to go. One path may be more painful than the other, but that doesn't mean it's to be avoided. All that matters is that you keep moving, fighting, working, struggling.

There will be discomfort in life. There will be sadness and pain. There will be bad days and bad moments. Like there were for me, there will be times when you are underestimated, discriminated against, counted out, cast aside. Systemic racism, gender discrimination, homophobia, religious bigotry, generational poverty—unfairness is in the DNA of our society. It's a fact. We plug away for change, but these things cannot be fixed overnight, and so you do your best to swim against the tide. If you're strong and fortunate enough to get to the other side, you stand up proudly. Then, you reach back and help those who are behind you, facing a similar struggle.

And therein lies the joy in life.

NEW YORK, JULY 2018

As I walk through the lobby and out into Times Square—into the pulsating mass of humanity, in the city I have always called home—it occurs to me that some days are better than others. Some days, in fact, are so good that you scarcely know how to process them. They seem, on the surface at least, to be the stuff of fantasy. This is one of those days.

A few minutes ago, I was on the phone with Brad Smith. The purpose of his call was to offer his congratulations on my promotion. With Brad's encouragement I had applied for the position of associate general counsel supporting global sales, marketing, and operations (GSMO), US regulated industries, which includes financial services, health, and life sciences, and the public sector group. The title is a mouthful, befitting its workload and strategic importance within one of the world's most prominent organizations. And now the job is mine. I will be overseeing a team of twenty legal professionals and leading the engagement of a $20 billion business.

More important, or at least of equal importance, is the fact that in this new role I will be supporting a division president who happens to be an African American woman. And the very thought of the improbability of that scenario—a Black female president, supported by a Black associate general counsel, in a company that, frankly, when I first arrived, could not have looked less like me—nearly brings me to tears.

There is more. I am trying to process all this while swimming across stream, navigating one of Midtown's busiest neighborhoods at rush hour on my way to the Port Authority Terminal and a subway ride back to my home in Brooklyn. I pause for a moment, take a few deep breaths. Summer in the city, and the air is thick and wet and pungent—an urban stew of car exhaust and food from street vendors and the sweat of a few million folks just trying to get through the day. I look around. So many people, all in their own little bubbles. I wonder if they see me. I wonder if they notice, and if they do, what do they think? A fiftysomething Black man walking out of an office building in Times Square, wearing sneakers, jeans, and a polo shirt—pushing the envelope on "business casual." Would they think he was a lead counsel at Microsoft? Or would they think he worked in the mailroom?

I smile and start to walk. At the intersection of Forty-First and Eighth, there is a blockade of people waiting for a chance to cross. My destination is dead ahead, but for some reason I look to the right. North. Uptown, so to speak. Roughly twenty blocks away are the Amsterdam Houses, and as I stare up Eighth Avenue, I am struck by the fact that it feels simultaneously to be both near and far—a literal mile from where I am standing, but a metaphorical world away.

The pedestrian light changes from red to white, and the crowd lurches forward. I am carried along with them, but on the other side, I pause again. I decide to turn right and head uptown, to check out the old neighborhood. This is something I do from time to time, both here and in Brooklyn, where I've also experienced poverty and comfort. I like to go back in time, to visit old friends and relatives, and to remind myself of where I came from.

It keeps me grounded. It keeps me sane. It reminds me that there is so much work still to be done when it comes to diversity and inclusion and social justice. I am living proof that America is a land of opportunity and promise, where anyone can rise above circumstances and turn dreams into reality. But I have experienced enough to know that hard work and determination are not always sufficient, that the playing field is woefully unlevel, and that in many ways, I am the exception that proves the rule. So, I do my part. And I don't forget.

I start walking up Eighth Avenue, insert a set of earbuds, and begin scrolling through the Spotify playlist on my phone, finally stopping at "Juicy," by the Notorious B.I.G.

> *Yeah, this album is dedicated*
> *To all the teachers that told me I'd never amount*
> *   to nothin'*
> *To all the people that lived above the buildings*
> *   that I was hustling in front of*

Then, it's on to Jay-Z, another New Yorker, singing "I Made It," both beating his chest in triumph and bowing down in gratitude to the friends and family who helped him and loved him along the way, and vowing always to take care of them. I shove my hands into my pockets and look at the asphalt and concrete, Eighth Avenue unwinding in the glint of the afternoon sun. I think about my grandmother, gone now, and what she would say if she could see me, and for a moment, the sadness rises in my throat. I choke it back down, turn up the volume, and push ahead. At once into the future . . . and into the past.

At Fifty-Ninth Street, I take a left and wander west for two blocks, turning north again at Amsterdam Avenue. Approaching 40 Amsterdam, the building where I once lived, I spot a familiar face. William. Still living in the projects, still trapped in the same old cycle. We walk together, chatting easily, in the way that people do when they've known each other forever. I met William in 1972, when I moved to the housing project. He was kind of an innocent kid whose mom would never let him hang out with me and my friends. We were a year or two older than William, and potentially a bad influence. She wanted to protect him, shelter him.

William tells me that he's returning to Amsterdam after some time away. Just got out of jail the previous day, in fact. He says this perfunctorily, without any noticeable sadness or regret or embarrassment. It is not a big deal. He's been incarcerated many times over the years, almost always for infractions related to possessing or selling narcotics. Or to carrying firearms, which is part of the deal when you sell drugs.

I ask for an update on some other folks in the neighborhood. *Dead*, William says in response to one name. *Prison* to another. *Fucked-up on drugs* to the rest.

We walk on for a few blocks, finally stopping at 50 Amsterdam Avenue, where William lives with his mother. The place is busy—people coming and going, kids playing outside. Different faces, same scene.

"Get your ass straight, man," I tell him. "You're too old for this nonsense."

He nods and says he will try. He starts to walk inside, then stops, turns.

"How are you doing?" he asks, almost as an afterthought.

"Hanging in there."

William smiles, says, "That's good," and then disappears.

I walk back across the street, heading toward the Sixty-Sixth Street subway station. I walk through Lincoln Center, past the Metropolitan Opera House and the Koch Theater, home of the NYC Ballet. I can see my twelve-year-old self running up to the line of taxis and fancy cars, pretending to be a valet. I see the patrons elegantly unfurl from their back seats, in their tuxedos and gowns, so neatly groomed, looking like money. Smelling like money.

You could see Lincoln Center from the Amsterdam Houses—you could see the lights twinkling and hear the sounds of sophistication—but it might as well have been on a different planet.

I walk into the subway station, head down the stairs, and swipe through the turnstiles. The platform is packed. Friday is the worst, of course. And the best. I put the earbuds back in and turn up the volume, Jay-Z's voice punching through the roar of the oncoming trains.

I'm a hold the fam down at least three generations
I'm talking when spaceships are around

and ya great, great grands . . .
Momma I made it

There is always unfinished business, the residue of history and family you can't quite wipe away or forget. Not long after I got that promotion, I visited my mother for dinner— she was still living in the Amsterdam Houses at the time, with my father an occasional houseguest. Sometimes, he'd stay for a few hours; other times, he'd stay for a few weeks. I'm not sure what brought them together or held them together after all these years—shared history, perhaps; lineage; or maybe just a desire for companionship.

My father remained a difficult personality: intelligent, antagonistic, self-righteous, and unstable. He and my mother fought often and loudly, until my father would storm out, or she'd grow tired of his irascibility, his drinking, and she'd ask him to leave, only to allow him to return after a period of cooling off. This had been the pattern for several years, and I'd been witness to it long enough to have developed a sense of detachment. If they wanted to continue this dance, that was their business—so long as no one got hurt. But I still had my own issues with John Wesley Miller, and, much as I tried to take the high road—to ignore his insults and provocations, the sound and the fury—sometimes we'd get into it, as well.

So it was on this particular night, when my father started in on my mother and then on my sister, who was also visiting. It was nothing out of the ordinary, just the usual poking and prodding, but for some reason, I found it more aggravating than usual.

"Stop running your mouth, Little Preacher," I said, using the nickname that had stuck after all these years, and which he still mostly found to be derogatory—particularly when coming from his son.

"What'd you say, boy?"

I stood up from the kitchen table, walked to where he was standing, and closed the distance between us to no more than a few feet. I was trying to control my temper, but I could feel the hair on the back of my neck standing up.

"I said shut up . . . Little Preacher."

My father was eighty-seven years old and carried about 140 pounds on a crooked five-and-a-half-foot frame. But he remained a fiery little guy who took no shit from anyone and, in fact, usually was the one doling out the shit.

"You motherfucker!" he shouted. "You want to fight? I will fuck you up!"

And with that, he lunged at me, his hands balled into tiny, wrinkled fists. I stepped to the side as he rushed past me and nearly fell to the floor, and suddenly the anger drained out of me, replaced by an urge to laugh.

"Come on, Dad. Take it easy." I extended a hand, at once a peace offering and an attempt to help him regain his balance.

"Fuck you!" he screamed, and then he charged at me again. "I'll kill you! And they won't do anything about it because I'm an old man. I can beat your ass and get away with it! Go ahead, call the cops!"

I raised my hands and backed away as my mother and my sister jumped between us and restrained him.

I could still hear him yelling as I walked out the door.

A few months passed. My mother told me she had kicked my father out of the house shortly after that incident, and while she wasn't willing to let him return, she was worried about his well-being. He was living in a shelter, she said, and it wasn't going well. He had been robbed. He wasn't eating.

"I'm sorry. What do you want me to do? He made his own bed a long time ago."

She nodded, said nothing.

"What is it, Mommy?"

"I was wondering if you would let him come live with you for a little while."

I found it very hard to say no to my mother, so instead of saying the first thought that popped into my head—*Are you crazy?!*—I said, "I'll think about it."

While I had no desire, and certainly no obligation, to rescue my father after a lifetime of estrangement and neglect, something pushed me toward the light of forgiveness and compassion. God had provided me with much more than I needed in life, much more than I thought I would ever have. What was to be gained through selfishness or, even worse, revenge? Would I somehow be happier knowing my father was living his final years in a shelter, when I had the means to care for him? Would that be retribution, and if so, who would be punished? My father, too old to really care, or to change, or to even understand what he had done and why he was so alone?

Or would I be the one who suffered, knowing I had deliberately added to his misery?

Would I be the one who was diminished?

My mother and siblings brokered the deal, explained to him the expectations for good behavior, for reining in the volatility and anger. He agreed. I offered to pick him up at the shelter in Queens, but he declined, saying he'd take the train. He showed up one afternoon, all his belongings—his entire life—packed into a single duffel bag. I showed him around the place, led him to his room. He sat on the edge of the bed, gave the mattress a judgmental push.

"Here's the way it's going to go," I said. "You're welcome to stay here. There will be rules, but I'm not going to treat you like a child. You'll have a place to stay. You'll be safe and comfortable. But you need to behave. You can't be flipping out on me, picking fights. I'm too old for that shit. And you're really too old for it."

He sat there stoically, listening, taking it in, periodically nodding in what I presumed to be reluctant agreement. And then this crusty old man, the father I barely knew and did not particularly like or even want to know, smiled.

"I have no problem with that, son," he said, the word startling in its intimacy. "Thank you."

We lived together for a while, surprisingly without incident. Then my mother moved in with us, and finally I moved out to another place and gave them the apartment, and they've lived together there, somewhat like a couple, albeit an unconventional one, for a couple years now, mostly free of acrimony and strife.

"I don't want to die in the projects," my mother used to say, as if it were a foregone conclusion. And now, she won't.

A while later, I sat down with my father and began asking him to share his life story. There were things I wanted to know, I explained. Things I needed to hear. Holes that needed filling.

"What for?" he asked grumpily.

"I'm writing a book."

"A book? About what?"

"My life." I paused. "And you're a part of that. Right? I mean, without you, there's no me."

He nodded.

"Damn right."

ACKNOWLEDGMENTS

I want to thank the many individuals who contributed to this memoir in one facet or another. First and foremost, I thank my entire family for contributing to my being. This book is dedicated to the wind beneath my wings: Flora Mae Miller, Mamie Jackson, Viola Jackson, my children, the late Ceola Harvell, and the late Ray "Spanky" Middleton.

I thank my parents for being true warriors. I extend a heartfelt thanks to my siblings for putting up with me: Robert Jackson, John Smith Jr., Diane Jackson, Jacqueline Brailsford, Maureen Miller, Vakeba Haynesworth, Essie Benton, and Tammy Benton. I wouldn't trade "Us" for the world.

I thank all my aunts, uncles, cousins, nieces, and nephews for the genuine love. It's reciprocated tenfold. I would like to especially thank the following cousins: Ernestine Jackson, Tasha Jackson, Phillip Jackson, Tee Lawton, Clarkson Wilson, Travis Wilson, and Mary Wilson. You've kept me smiling on so many occasions when I needed it the most.

To my children: Sabree, Maya, Kayla, and Corey. Thanks for letting me be your dad and never being impressed with anything I say or do. To Katherine (Kat) Rodriguez, my loving partner: thank you for your patience and tolerance. The unconditional love and support from everyone is priceless.

I thank all my friends from the Amsterdam Houses projects in New York City. *I am never far from home*, and you are always in my thoughts. I especially thank Clayton Anges, Alejandro Nazario, Lori Thompson, and Veronica Spann for the camaraderie and great memories.

To my dear friend: the late Ray "Spanky" Middleton— your true friendship and staunch support will be sorely missed. I will always cherish the memories. Rest well.

I carry a special torch for all my brothers of the MALIK Fraternity, Inc. and all the brothers from the TAA Chapter. I thank my line brothers: Melvin Boone, Sabir Mateen, Tariq Kareem Shabazz, Erskine Isaac, and our pledge captain, the late David J. Nelson. You all have contributed significantly to the man I have become. Our bond is real. Special thanks to Erskine for always being available when I need a photographer.

To the NOAH program and the entire NOAH family at Hofstra University—especially Frank Smith and Pat McCracken. Your guidance and commitment to excellence helped pave the way for my higher education and upward mobility. I am forever grateful.

Thank you to Georgetown Law School. Special thanks to Dean Wilmot, Dean Miller, Dean Bellamy, and Sam Harvey. My legal aptitude is solid because of you all. A special thanks to my law school classmate and best friend David Green. Thank you for being true-blue and one of the best attorneys I know. We pressed through so much together.

Thank you to my Martin Luther King Jr. High School friends and family. Thank you to my Baruch College family and students. Being a professor was a wonderful experience for me.

Thank you to Denise Brown for introducing me to Kendall Minter and being a loyal friend. I thank Kendall Minter and Darrell Gay for giving me the opportunity to gain experience and for opening the door to the entertainment industry.

To my comrades at the law offices of Jackson, Brown, Powell, and St. George. Together, we kicked down the entertainment industry doors, and I would not have wanted it any other way. Clifford Brown, Johan Powell, and Norman St. George—I salute you. Thanks for joining me on an incredible ride. Thanks, Clifford, for the late-night advice. We could not have done it without the support and dedication of Magda Vives, Jerry Juste, and Denyce Price Jackson. Denyce, you made it possible for me to develop the firm into what it became.

Thank you to our clients who made me better at my craft. A special thanks to our clients Tony Dofat and Pete Rock & CL Smooth for contributing to our firm's growth. Word of mouth is powerful!

Thank you to the National Association of Minority and Women Owned Law Firms for allowing me to serve. Thank you to Mary Snapp for placing me on the diversity committee and advisory board. It's an honor and privilege to serve in this capacity. I would not be where I am at today without the help of so many diverse women.

Thank you to the many organizations and bar associations that I belong to and that have always supported me.

Special thanks to the Minority Corporate Counsel Association. Your work has propelled many attorneys. Keep going strong.

Thank you to Rocky Bucano and the Universal Hip Hop Museum team. I am proud to be a part of this board and the launching of this monumental project. I could not think of a better way to stay connected to my hip hop roots.

Thank you to the Henry Street Settlement for all that you do and for allowing me to help open doors of opportunity for the underserved in New York City. May blessings continue to flow your way.

Thank you to Mayor Eric Adams for appointing me to his corporate council committee and allowing me to serve the great people of New York City. Thank you to the past governor David Paterson for allowing me to serve great people across the state of New York.

A heartfelt thank-you to the following friends, advisers, and mentors: Sincere Thompson of Frontline Marketing, Les Bailey, Ray Chick, Sylvia Rhone, Clarence Avant, the late Andre Harrell, Mel Lewinter, Charles Fisher, Hip-Hop Summit Youth Council (HHSYC), and Paul Martin. Thank you for the encouragement and believing in me throughout the years. Thank you to the entire team behind the scenes—you know who you are. You are all phenomenal!

Special thanks to Ameena Ali of Y3K Innovations for being the engine for communications, sales, promotion, and marketing—your guidance, creativity, and execution are impeccable. Special thanks to the talent who helped make this book possible: Dan Pearson/Dan 4 Entertainment for his management and bringing everyone together. Joe Layden for his editorial guidance and helping me pull together the threads of my life story and tie them into one narrative. Frank Weimann, Folio Literary Management, for being an incredible agent; Nicholas Ciani for his vision and Denise Gibbon for her help. Thank you to the Atria/Simon & Schuster family. Thank you all for extending your literary gifts.

A very special thanks to my second set of eyes on this project: Katherine Rodriguez and Clemon (Clem) Richardson. Your attention to detail is impeccable. Thank you for your input. I also want to thank you for your general advice and guidance.

To my Microsoft family: Casia Thaniel, Valecia Maclin, Neal Suggs, Marc Waters, Fred Humphries, Daphne Forbes, Jay Jackson, Elke Suber, Aileen O'Brien, Sonya Johnston, Adrienne Williams, and Toni Townes-Whitley. Thank you, Lisa Tanzi, for hiring me. Where did the years go? I thank you for the ongoing support and teamwork.

An incredibly special thanks to Brad Smith and Carol Ann Browne for their leadership, friendship, unwavering support, and sharing of knowledge.

I especially thank every diversity, equity, and inclusion advocate working across the board. It is time to level the playing field.

If I have missed anyone, please do not charge it to my heart. I am grateful for everyone I have ever encountered throughout this journey called life. This memoir is my way of saying that I, too, believe in you. Never give up!

ABOUT THE AUTHOR

BRUCE JACKSON is an associate general counsel for Microsoft, where he supports the US global sales, marketing, and operations group, leading the engagement of a $20 billion business and managing a team of more than twenty. Jackson began his career at Microsoft in 2000 as corporate counsel for the digital media division. He brought a broad and unique skill set to Microsoft as a highly acclaimed entertainment attorney who represented an extensive list of hip hop royalty during the 1990s. Since then, he has received Microsoft's diversity award, participated in Microsoft's law and corporate affairs' diversity efforts, helped launch Microsoft's Elevate America veterans' initiative, and works within Microsoft to develop its diverse recruitment pipeline. Jackson sits on the New York City Mayor's Corporate Council, was appointed to New York State's Advisory Council on Interactive Media and Youth Violence by former governor David Paterson, and is a board member of the Universal Hip Hop Museum in the Bronx, New York. Jackson received a BBA in public accounting from Hofstra University and a JD and an LLM in taxation from Georgetown University Law Center. He is a doting dad to three daughters and one son.